Edi

For most of us, th
chocolate are as
memories of one's … particularly to childhood. But there's more to chocolate than these sentimental considerations: what do we know about the healing properties of chocolate? What's the real history of cocoa and how is that foodstuff used in cuisine? Which are the different stages a cocoa bean goes through before being transformed into a chocolate bar? The Guide to Belgian Chocolate will reveal you everything you could wish to know about that precious substance.

Is it really necessary to underline the importance of Belgium in the field of chocolate making? Everywhere in the world, Belgian chocolate is renowned for its high quality and delightful taste. In these pages you'll discover the most famous Belgian chocolate makers and the history of their rise, but also some more recent establishments. Still not famous worldwide yet, they bring a breath of originality to the chocolate world, with their daring associations of flavours, and are already much appreciated in Belgium!

Time has come to devour this guide, following the numerous paths that lead to chocolate…

Table of contents

Did you know it?

The first book entirely dedicated to chocolate was published in Mexico in 1609. Its title: "Book dealing with chocolate". It certainly looked quite different from the book you're holding in your hands right now!

The typical chocolate consumer is a man, aged between 18 and 34, with the profile of the yuppie. Housewives and students come respectively second and third.

Did you know that every Belgian consumes about 8 kg of chocolate per year, which corresponds to 25% more than the American?

40F
REPUBLIQUE TOGOLAISE

50F
REPUBLIQUE TOGOLAISE

Le Petit Futé Guide to Belgian Chocolate - Registration of copyright 3rd quarter 2001
Publisher: NEOCITY sprl - rue Geleytsbeek, 168 - 1180 Bruxelles
Tel: 32 (0)2 374 63 84 - Fax: 32 (0)2 374 71 82
e-mail: petitfute@wanadoo.be - Web: www.petitfute.com

Director of publishing: Philippe Wyvekens
Author: Bernard Dubrulle
Translation: Erik Poole and Isabelle Collard
Administration : Marie Lasource
Composition : MK Partners sprl - 4260 Braives - Tel. 019 69 72 74 - Belgium
Photoengraving: Vreven sprl - 4257 Berloz - Tel. 32 (0)19 33 87 87 - Belgium
Printing: Corlet printing - France

For the photographs, acknowledgements to:
Barry Callebaut, Corné Food, Corné Van Parys, Côte d'Or, Duc d'O, Galler, Godiva, Guylian, Italo-Suisse, Jacques, Lindt, Neuhaus, Passion Chocolat, Pierre Marcolini, Valrhona, Weiss.

The Petit Futé was founded by Dominique Auzias (Nouvelles Editions de l'Université - Paris).

The history of chocolate

In 1502, as Christopher Columbus was setting foot in the Americas, the natives offered him a bowl of chocolate as a welcoming gift. At that time, no one knew that cocoa would reach a position of capital importance in world commerce. Columbus, preoccupied with his search for a route to the Indies, made note of the fact that the indigenous peoples used it both as a drink and as a medium of currency, but he remained completely disinterested.

Christopher Columbus discovers America... and chocolate!

The Pre-Columbian Era

We must go back to the year 400 to find the first traces of cocoa bean consumption. The Mayas, whose territory supported the growth of cocoa trees, probably first saw monkeys consuming it, eating the white fleshy pulp that surrounds the beans themselves, the beans being too bitter to consume as they exist naturally.

We do not know precisely how they hit upon the idea of letting the beans ferment, nor how they thought to roast them. Nonetheless, cocoa rapidly conquered the neighbouring cultures: the Toltecs, then the Aztecs who subjugated them, and made a true cult of cocoa. According to them, Quetzlcoatl, the king and priest, was considered like a living god because he had taught his subjects to cultivate cocoa.

Over the centuries, the people that would become known as "Indians" brewed cocoa from a dense paste made from roasted cocoa beans. With the addition of water and various spices (vanilla and cinnamon, but also pepper and other strong condiments), it became a very popular beverage drunk by kings as well as their poorest subjects. The poorest however, used it to merely flavour a boiled corn mixture.

Cocoa as Currency

Cocoa beans being so highly coveted, it was only natural that they would become currency. The Spaniard Oviedo y Valdez noted in a report from 1513 that a slave could be purchased for 100 beans. Note also that cocoa was a sort of "unique currency", like the Euro, with a value regardless of territory or ethnicity of the holder.

The Maya and Aztec cocoa cult was so deeply sanctified that they used it in rituals for every-

Representation dating from the pre-Colombian era

thing from birth to death, when they placed a sufficient quantity of cocoa in tombs to accompany the departed on their last voyage.

In 1519, the navigator Hernan Cortès landed on the coast of Tabasco (author's note : not lacking in spice of its own) with the intention of conquering the territory. He was greeted by the representatives of king Montezuma, who saw in him the foretold reincarnation of Quetzlcoatl. He was venerated and covered with gold, so much so in fact, that Cortès and his men had no trouble in seizing the coveted territory. As a gift, he received, in addition to his accommodation, a vast plantation of cocoa trees. We suppose that the value attributed to cocoa helped to catch the attention of the Spaniards ; their goal in the beginning probably being to exchange it for gold.

We need a small sidebar here to note the vast wisdom of Quetzlcoatl. He announced that he would return in a future century, as he left the region in disgrace, along with a few others like him. We see that up until today, this reappearance hasn't happened, but we can't help but think of the arrival of Cortès in the XVIth century as a sort of temporary comeback.

The Arrival of Chocolate in Europe

In 1528, Cortès returned to Spain with a cargo of cocoa beans, production materials, and the recipe for making chocolate. This was cocoa's formal entry

Cocoa, a highly-coveted foodstuff

onto the European continent. In reality, King Ferdinand II of Aragon had already received some by way of Christopher Columbus, but was uninterested. Even so, it took until 1580 for the Spaniards to really embrace this new foodstuff. That was the year of the creation of the first chocolate manufacturer on Iberian soil, and when the importation of cocoa beans really took off. The addition of cane sugar, in addition to and in place of, spices was without a doubt the detonator : cocoa had become a beverage that was sweet and agreeable to drink.

In this period Spain possessed territories in many regions all over the world, including the Netherlands which were acquired through inheritance. So, it was completely natural for chocolate to traverse the borders of Spain. The history of chocolate in Belgium begins thusly in 1635, near Ghent. Even in those days, it was given as a gift from the monks of an abbey.

It all started in Spain...

A few years earlier, in 1615, chocolate made its first appearance at the court of the king of France, when Louis XIII married Anne d'Autriche, infanta of ... Spain. In the following generation, with Louis XIV and Marie-Thérèse d'Autriche, she too of Spanish heritage, the phenomenon only deepened. And so, the first French chocolate manufacturer was founded in 1659 and was named David Chaillou. It received a royal authorization to "*make, sell and retail a composition known as chocolate.*" At this time, the fabrication process was still relatively simple. The beans were hulled manually, roasted, then ground in a mortar.

Nonetheless, the beginnings of chocolate in France are surrounded by some controversy. Some say that Lyon would have been the first trans-Pyrenean stop for chocolate, by way of Alphonse, the brother of cardinal Richelieu, while the most recent legend holds that it was Jews chased from Spain who, settling in Bayonne, introduced cocoa into France in 1609. Even today the Basque city is considered the capital of French chocolate.

Outside of the Iberian peninsula, cocoa also landed in Italy in 1606, thanks to a Florentine merchant. Other sources site a voyage to the Antilles around 1600. Navigators would have also found the celebrated beans, and could have returned with them to Italy. From there, cocoa conquered Austria in 1640 and Germany in 1713. As for the British Isles, they discovered chocolate in 1657, when a Frenchman established himself there with his own recipes.

This phenomenon was no doubt part of the ever increasing enrichment of Spain, as demand was growing without limit. Because, for the period of a century, all of the cocoa growing regions of the earth were possessions of Spain. Their hegemony was brought to an end when England took possession of the Antilles.

19th century dissertation about chocolate.

The Industrial Era

The first manufacturer of significant size was created in Barcelona in 1780. The same year, in Bayonne, a strange machine made its debut. It was a steam engine, designed to grind and mix the paste. Chocolate thereby entered into a new phase, one of industrial production. This delicious beverage that had seduced all the royal

Post sleigh in the Tyrolean Alps

courts of Europe had also propagated itself among the bourgeoisie : it had left the royal salons and penetrated into the upper crust of society, where everything that is in vogue has its moment in the sun. From this moment on, chocolate was no longer just a fad phenomenon ...
Mechanisation allowed chocolate production to be envisioned at much higher levels. The first factory worthy of that appellation was created in 1815 by the Dutchman Van Houten, to whom we owe the process of separation of powder from the cocoa butter, discovered in 1828. A small revolution : this technique permitted the fatty materials to be set aside and allowed the cocoa to be ground more finely.
Improvements in the manufacturing process came from all parts. An engineer named Poincelet invented, in 1811, a mixer that was rapidly adopted all over Europe. Around 1850, Mélinans introduced in Lyon a process to simultaneously grind and mix while the roaster was performing its task.

Rodolphe Lindt

During the same period, science began to take an interest in cocoa. The Swedish naturalist Karl Von Linné gave it a scientific denomination in 1734 and named it *Theobroma cocoa*, which humbly means "food of the gods". In 1841, a Russian chemist isolated *theobromine* and discovered some of its properties.

Chocolate takes its shape(s)

In addition to the evolution of technique and a certain democratisation,

Henri Nestlé

chocolate still had major advances ahead. It would benefit, through the XVIIIth and XIXth centuries, from the inventiveness of chocolate makers of all nations. It would no longer be confined to the role of a beverage, though certain other forms already existed (as pastilles, sugar covered or *"Spanish"* sausages).

And so, the first chocolate with hazel nuts appeared in 1830, thanks to the Swiss Charles-Amédée Kohler, while in 1847 the Fry confectionary of Bristol created the first eating chocolate. The following year Auguste Poulain made the first bar of chocolate in his factory in Blois and in 1875 Daniel Peter, another Swiss, dreamt up the idea of adding milk, thanks to a condensation process initiated by Henri Nestlé. Four years later, in 1879, Rodolphe Lindt delivered chocolate *de couverture*, of which some still make a specialty today, and discovered the process of *conching*. We also owe chocolate fondue to him.

Over these two centuries, the Spanish registered their slow but irreversible disinterest in chocolate specialties. While in the XVIIIth century they still consumed one third of the world production of cocoa, and they were the first to consume it in a solid form, this tendency reversed itself fairly quickly and they relinquished their leader's position to other countries, like Switzerland, Belgium or France.

The XXth Century

The industrialisation of chocolate making definitely had some beneficial side effects. The costs of production were greatly reduced, which allowed all levels of society to enjoy chocolate. Among them, children rapidly became a private niche market

Meurisse's stand at the World Fair(Brussels, 1910).

for chocolate makers. Marketing, or even simple advertising, allowed them to attract and retain this market sector, notably with the help of characters and small toys.

The train of novelties didn't stop either, and other types of products came to light. In 1923, the American Franck Mars launched the *Milky-Way*, while his son invented the bar that carries his name, the *Mars Bar*. Today we can count a multitude of variations on this theme.

Chocolate spreads, like *Nutella*, also made their appearance in most homes at this time, while the consumption of chocolate became more generalised and stretched into many other sectors of foodstuffs. Who can, in today's world, claim to have never eaten or drunk chocolate in one form or another ?

A return to luxury status ?

In contrast, this turn of the century finds us amidst a new public preoccupation with quality chocolates. There are many makers who have launched products that are more costly, but whose irreproachable quality aims to create an image like the specialized foreign producers.

In this niche we place *Galler* from Belgium, whose distribution has succeeded equally well from large stores and from specialised boutiques. In France, the master-confectioners, like Robert Linxe (*La Maison du Chocolat*) or *Bernard Dufoux*, have succeeded, due to their passion and incessant research, in raising their production to the summit of the international hierarchy. In bringing to the Pantheon a dark chocolate, very strong and rich in cocoa, they have lifted chocolate from the niche " kid's stuff " market and

The new quality label for chocolate, initiated by the Belgian government

transformed it into a product prized by adults. As for the Swiss, we regret that their most famous chocolates are also their most industrial, but that overlooks that on the world scale, they still wear jersey number 1 when it comes to renown.

But, for many years, chocolate has also been politicised. In this

The chocolate seller

arena, the year 2000 will definitely qualify as " historic ". In June, The European Parliament decided to weigh in on a growing debate that goes back to 1973. At that time, the Common Market was composed of six member states: France, Belgium, Luxembourg, The Netherlands, Germany and Italy. Among them, the latter three claimed authorization to use vegetable fats other than cocoa butter. The debate was delayed, and European politics hasn't stopped growing.

Regularly brought to the table, the discussion found a resolution recently : producers are henceforth allowed to use a maximum of 5% vegetable fats other than cocoa. Alone against the twelve others, France, Belgium and Luxembourg were unable to tilt the balance in their favour.

Ambao, that's good chocolate !

Belgian confectioners announced immediately that they would not adhere to this new European directive and the government encouraged the creation of a " Belgian chocolate" label to distinguish it from other creations less " ethically correct " It was presented to the public a fine Sunday in October 2000 and was baptised *Ambao*.

Along the same lines, researchers from the CUL (Catholic University of Louvain) have just made a " chocolate detector " that can sense the presence of other vegetable fats.

Beyond the unhealthy protectionism, we can push the debate a notch further. What about the cocoa producing countries ? How will they deal with the inevitable drop in demand ? The partisans of the 5% cause retort that these regions also cultivate the plants from which these infamous vegetable fats are extracted. Probably, but we must underline the fact that up to the present, there exists no list of authorised oils. And although the " recommended " mixture contains 50% shea butter (whose principle producers are also situated in West Africa), it does not exclude in any way the use, in part or in total, of palm oil, a clearly less costly alternative for chocolate makers.

Still, the consumer could read the packaging, which must include specific mention of the addition of other vegetable fats. But in practice, and in the absence of rules for this mention, this runs the very real risk of being lost among a sea of other annotations. We could find ourselves in a closely analogous situation to tobacco, where every smoker knows the counter-indications printed on the cigarette packaging by heart and they no longer pay any attention.

The debate isn't really closed, and the dawning XXIst century will certainly bring us its own lot of surprises....

Charlie and the chocolate factory, a classic of children litterature.

Chocolate among the famous people

Chocolate is probably the only solid foodstuff that has engendered such passion or revulsion, in any age. And though it's a fairly regular commodity in our lives, public personalities, from all areas and ages, have also frequently shared their feelings about chocolate. So here is a little peek into what those famous men and women have said or written on the subject.

While preparing for his voyage to Switzerland, the German philosopher Goethe packed into his bags a sufficient amount of chocolate, because he didn't have much faith in ... Swiss chocolate! He liked chocolate so much he once exclaimed that, *"Whoever drinks a cup of chocolate can withstand a day of travel "*.

Queen Marie-Thérèse d'Autriche, wife of Louis XIV, was an unwavering supporter of chocolate. She even said : *"I have two passions, the King and chocolate "*.

The writer Honoré de Balzac discovered, before scientists, that chocolate maintains wakeful cerebral activity for a longer time. Turning this around, he stated that : *"Who knows if the abuse of chocolate might have had something to do with the downfall of the Spanish nation..."*.

We ascribe to the Marquise de Sévigné a turn of phrase that makes us laugh today : *« The Marquise de Coëtlogon ate so much chocolate that, being pregnant, she gave birth to a little boy as black as the devil, so black that he died of it...".*

As for the genial gourmet Brillat-Savarin, he is one of the most verbose flatterers on the subject of chocolate. We ascribe to him a series of maxims on the subject, more or less well known, including : *" Happy chocolate who, after travelling the globe, traverses the smile of a woman and finds death in a savoury kiss, melting in their mouth".* Something less well known is this reply, made by the mother superior of the convent of Belley in the French department of Ain: *"Chocolate must be prepared the night before in order to make it smooth ...".*

The very arousing Marquis de Sade, as if to reinforce the rumours, offered to the ladies of Marseille, where he was hosting a ball, chocolate pastilles filled with cantharis, a potent aphrodisiac.

Closer to us, an ad showed the painter Salvador Dali claiming that he was "crazy for Lanvin chocolate", though no trace is found in his canvases. This theme was recently repeated by the brand, who this time featured the ineffable Stéphane Bern.

As for Philippe Geluck, father of the famous *Chat* (Belgian comic strip) and ubiquitous talk-show member, his parents said of him "that he would sell his soul to the devil for chocolate". He probably did a lot better than that by loaning his image to Jean Galler.

And, though it is impossible to review all the books, songs or films where chocolate plays a role, we couldn't resist mentioning the first version of *Cigars of the Pharaoh* where Tintin saves himself from a sticky situation thanks to ... a bar of chocolate !!

To conclude, take note that although celebrities may love chocolate, it gives a little back to them, as well : a French confectioner even marketed a line of chocolaty sweets named ... the *Giscards*.

Chabrol's production for 2000: "Thank you for the chocolate".

Cocoa

Producing countries

Contrary to what one might think, cocoa originates uniquely on the American continent. Although since the 1970's the principal producers in the world market have been grouped in western Africa, with the Ivory Coast being far in the lead, the introduction of cocoa to the African continent was a feat of the Europeans. To whit, it was the Portuguese Jose Ferreira Gomes who planted cocoa in 1822 on a small island in the gulf of Guinea. The Lusitanian navigator, wishing simply to make a gift of an ornamental plant to Africa, probably had no idea of the impact of his gesture. The development of African colonies would take care of the rest ....

On the other hand, Gomes had far reaching vision as far as the appropriate atmospheric conditions for the development of the cocoa tree. In fact, it grows exclusively in a zone from the 15th North parallel to the 15th South parallel : what is sometimes called the "cocoa belt". The plant demands a humid climate (around 100 inches of rain per year), shade and heat, where the average temperature stabilises around 77°F. The ideal altitude is somewhere between 1300 and 2000 feet.

The Ivory Coast, uncontested leader

Today, cultivation of cocoa takes place in three different zones (Africa, Asia and South America), among which about 60% comes from Africa alone, and 11% from Brazil, still losing steam as compared to the production during the 80's. As a comparison, note that in 1810, Venezuela supplied about half of the total cocoa demand.

The increasing development of plantations in South-East Asia seems very promising, especially thanks to research into higher yield production methods. In this region, Indonesia emerges in front, with 10% of the world production. As for the introduction of the plant into this part of the world, that traces back to Pedro Bravo de los Camerinos, a Spanish sailor, who abandoned his activities as a conquistador in 1670 and introduced cocoa to the Philippines.

For the local populations, cocoa cultivation often represents one of the principle sources of revenue and, as is the case for coffee and other major food crops, cocoa is subject to pointed negotiations with the importing countries. Cooperatives have been organized in some countries, like the Ivory Coast, in order to protect the interests of the smaller producers.

As for purists, true amateurs and chocolate aficionados, they search for cocoa from Venezuela, Trinidad or Ecuador. The quantities produced there are relatively small, but the fine aroma of the beans is unequalled.

The different varieties of cocoa

There are three botanical varieties of cocoa called *forasteros*, *criollos* and *trinitarios*, each with their own characteristics

Ripe cocoa fruits.
Beneath, a cocoa tree.

and with their own sub-divisions called *"crus"* (appellations). As with grape vines, each is influenced by the conditions where it is grown, the soil, sunlight, ...

The *forasteros* are the most popular variety, making up about 70% of production. It yields a cocoa for everyday consumption : the plant is vigorous, an excellent producer, and the beans give a flavour that is acidic and full bodied. They are found principally in Brazil and western Africa, though it originated in the upper Amazon. Its resistant characteristics sometimes lead to the name *robusta*, by analogy to the coffee tree. These beans are used mainly for milk chocolate and cocoa powder. Among the principle appellations are the *Maragnan* and the *Arriba*.

The *criollos* make up about 8% of total production. This variety is the lowest producer in terms of quantity and the variety with the most fragile beans. Connoisseurs aren't shy about singing the praises of its fine aroma and mild flavour, the most noble and costly. It is almost exclusively used in luxury chocolates and its cultivation is all but unique to Venezuela. Growers also use it to create new varieties to be grown in Asia. The most used appella-

tions are the *Sambirano*, the *Puerto Cabello*, the *Chuao*, and the *Indonesian criollo*.

Finally, the *trinitarios* (named for the island of Trinidad) are the offspring of a cross between the two previous varieties. They offer optimal production while the flavour is fine and the beans hold a high amount of fats. The level of production is estimated at 20% of the world total. Its excellent characteristics make it the variety preferred by growers, who tend to substitute it more and more for the *forasteros*. The best *trinitarios* are the *Santa Severa* and the *Java*, which specialists sometime call the *Médoc of Cocoa*.

From a strictly commercial point of view, the beans are separated into two distinct categories : *noble cocoa* and *cocoa for daily consumption*, in function of the quantities offered for sale.

A highly courted bean

But outside of these specifics, essentially gustative and economic, the different varieties of cocoa have similar characteristics. The beans are contained within pods, a sort of large fruit similar to a gourd. Their colour, running from yellow to reddish-brown depending on their state of ripeness, offers no clue to which variety they may belong.

These pods grow on cocoa trees once they have reached maturity; that is when they've reached an age of eight years. The first flowers appear when the tree reaches its fifth year. The cocoa tree can easily reach a height of 50 feet and an average age of 60 years. It benefits from the shade necessary to ripen its fruits, thanks to other trees taller than it, politely called the "mothers of the cocoa". However, its height is often limited to around 20 feet, essentially to facilitate harvesting that must always be done by hand in order to preserve the fragile fruits. A rarity among other species, the fruits grow directly on the trunks of the cocoa tree.

Each tree fruits twice per year and a single tree will show different stages of flowering and fruiting. Nonetheless, productivity is fairly limited, for the 50.000 to 100.000 annual flowers on a tree, only 5% will be pollinated. And, of the small percentage of fruits that will result, around 30 pods will contain the sought after beans, numbering 25 to 50 per pod. On average then, a tree supplies from 3 to 4.5 lbs of beans per year.

We can easily understand from this the stake required for cultivation of cocoa, the prices made in the international market place ... and the nickname given to the beans : *brown gold*.

From the plantation to the export port

The harvest

The harvest takes place from October to March, at different times according to the region. It is accomplished with the help of very sharp knives, attached to long poles. The pods, even when ripe, almost never fall from the tree, so it is important to proceed with the cutting at just the right moment. Once the pods are cut from the tree, when they are 4 or 5 months old, they are carefully split open vertically in order to extract the beans within. These are found among a white pulpy substance that must be removed, easily done if the appropriate stage of ripeness has been reached.

The fermentation

Fermentation is probably the most important step of those performed in the producing countries. It lasts from 3 to 7 days, depending on the type of bean. In this stage, enzymes will be activated and allow the beans to acquire their particular flavour while losing some of their bitterness. Above all, they stop the phenomenon of germination by "killing" the seeds. Paradoxically, it is the most delicate beans (*criollos*) that ferment the quickest.

For centuries, this operation has been accomplished in the traditional manner by laying the seeds on large leaves, for example banana leaves. The tropical climate and the energy of the sun engender the fermentation process. Any remaining mucilage dries and falls from the cocoa seeds. As in all fermentation, oxygen is critical to the process : this is provided by regularly stirring the beans. The pulp transforms into alcohol under the action of the yeasts and the alcohol is in turn transformed into acetic acid. From this moment the beans have their characteristic brown colour and have fixed their definitive aroma of chocolate.

Inside of a cocoa fruit.

Modernisation of the technique

Henceforth, the seeds, now dead, may carry the name of cocoa bean. They will swell to their full size as the fermentation continues for another day or two.

Today, the banana leaf technique has almost disappeared, especially among mid to large size businesses. It is often replaced by a system of wooden boxes or crates, perforated, and laid out next to one another, usually in a stair step fashion, the newer seeds placed in the higher beds. The seeds change containers each day, this process offers the advantage of removing the need to stir the contents of the containers, since oxygen is provided during the move.

Before moving on to the next stage, we will present a small sidebar in order to make a comparison that is somewhat stronger than it may seem at first.

We can easily draw a parallel between cocoa and coffee, two tropical plants, with fairly similar methods of cultivation and transformation. Both undergo fermentation, which takes place at the same point in the processing of each, that is, before drying. In both cases it serves to interrupt the germination phenomenon. On the other hand, barley, and to a certain extent wheat - characteristic crops of the northern hemisphere - are two of the principle ingredients in beer as it is produced in Europe and North America. In this case, fermentation is a step in the brewing process, but it takes place on barley that has already germinated and been roasted, which we call malt.

The drying

Drying provides a definite end to the process of fermentation in the cocoa beans. This operation lasts 5 to 7 days and is the last to take place in the producing country. Here again two different methods are used depending on the type of production.

The traditional technique consists of spreading the beans over a large flat surface, mats, screens or directly on the ground. They are left under the rays of the sun and arranged in layers 2 to 4 inches thick. The cocoa is stirred regularly by hand in order to allow the ambient air to assist in the drying and to avoid the appearance of unwanted moulds. Along the same line of thinking, the method used in Brazil consists of arranging the beans on huge concrete slabs where the natives stir them with their bare feet. They say that this gives the beans a beautiful golden colour.

When the best is the enemy of good...

The "modern" method consists of spreading the beans in large machines, shaded from sunlight. The drying is then accomplished by the action of a fire that raises the temperature (to around 212 to 250°F) and lowers the humidity level. Though this method has the advantages of speeding the process and protecting it from certain weather hazards, it interferes with the flavour of the beans since they become impregnated with a smoky taste and do not benefit from a supplemental flavour enhancement due to the additional sunlight of the traditional method.

Producers take advantage of the drying period to separate the beans according to their grade and to set aside those unfit for consumption. Also, the harvest is considered successful

Cocoa beans ready for exportation

Traditional drying methods

if it reaches 40% of the total mass of the fresh seeds. During this operation, the moisture content of the beans passes from 60% to 6%, the upper limit which can not be broken without risk of moulds.

Finally, last but not least, drying refines the particular qualities of each of the different varieties of cocoa.

The export

Once graded, the cocoa is stocked in large jute sacks, holding from 130 to 200 lbs. These sacks preserve the beans from the humidity and parasites, of which the *monilia* fungus can ruin an entire harvest. These events are fairly common at the depots where the sacks await their departure to the countries of chocolate production. On that point, the partitioning of the harvests is fairly clear cut, since Brazil supplies mostly the United States (whose most famous chocolates in Europe are called *Mars*, *Milky-Way* or *Snickers*), while Africa essentially provisions Europe.

The cocoa market is negotiated, in the manner of other merchandise (sugar or coffee for example), before the harvest arrives at the depots, sometimes even while the fruit is still on the trees. It functions along the lines of a futures market. The main markets are in New York, Paris and London. The prices are fixed as a function of supply and demand, grade, quality of beans, and quantities purchased. The current tendency is toward a stabilisation, unfortunately, in the favour of the importing countries.

Among these, the principles are of course in Europe, which imports 60% of the world production (a number that is of course related to the world export market share garnered by Africa), while Belgium alone captures 6%.

Pressing of the cocoa beans in Brazil

MERCI
ZACK

Chocolate

The stages of production

Once the cocoa arrives in its destination country, a series of operations more complex than they appear are necessary to transform the bean into delicious chocolate.

Selection and cleaning

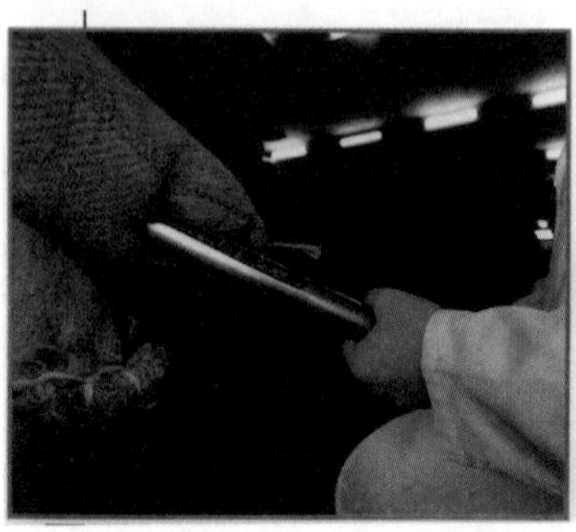

Selection of the cocoa beans in a chocolate factory

The cocoa bean being very fragile, the first step, before all else, consists of a rigorous selection process in order to remove all those that have any symptoms of poor quality. This might be caused by insufficient fermentation, foreign residues on the beans or incomplete drying.

Once this operation is completed, the cocoa beans are placed in large silos to await use. This allows them to be held in optimal conditions : the temperature and humidity are constantly monitored and sufficient aeration is provided as necessary.

Just before their transformation – and only then – the beans are removed from the silo to undergo a last verification of their condition. It is also at this moment that the beans' fat content is determined in the laboratory.

Roasting

This is surely one of the most important phases of the transformation. The chocolate maker starts by drying the beans to bring their water content down to 3%. Next, they will be heated to a temperature of 250 to 265°F, depending on the type of bean. This operation lasts from 15 to 35 minutes according to the depth of roasting wanted and determines the colour and the aroma of the chocolate. It all takes place in spherical drums that continually rotate. During the roasting, the beans lose from 5 to 15% of their weight. Prudence is the rule of thumb : too intense a heat or left too long the beans will burn, while an acidity or too much bitterness often has at its origin too low a roasting temperature.

Two techniques exist : one roasts the beans whole with their hull intact, the other hulled and ground beforehand.

From an equipment point of view, the more technologically advanced enterprises use processes completely managed by computer.

Production of cocoa liquor

Still, in one sense, the making of chocolate is very much the same. For instance, once the roasting reaches the desired point, the chocolate maker places the beans into a grinder. The seeds are separated from their hull and are reduced to a course paste called cocoa liquor (in French *grué* or *nibs*).

Chocolate is often composed of a mixture of beans coming from

different varieties of cocoa tree (as is done with grapes from different vine stock for winemaking). This "assembly" takes place at this stage of the production and allows the chocolate to procure the desired flavour.
Next, after a final quality control, the cocoa liquor is ground down further until a compact paste is obtained.

Transformation of the cocoa.

Finally chocolate

Needless to bring up again, one of the principle elements of chocolate in addition to the finished product is of course *cocoa butter*. It is a material rich in fine oils that give good chocolate its breaking and melting characteristics. For this reason, during the mixing operation, a little more is added in addition to that contained naturally in the beans.
Other ingredients also enter into the making of chocolate.
Sugar is indispensable. It allows the cocoa to fully release its aromas. And if it is disallowed for medical reasons, it may be replaced by fructose, maltose or *maltitol*. But, too great a proportion of sugar will cover the essential aromas of the cocoa.
Powdered *milk* would be added if one decides to make milk chocolate.
Even though it is not truly indispensable, *soy lecithin* is almost systematically added (to bind the ingredients to one another), as well as *vanilla* extract.
Next, the chocolate maker proceeds to a second grinding, destined to give the chocolate the necessary fineness characteristic of Belgian and French chocolates. The resulting paste is heated and briskly agitated : from one side runs the cocoa butter, and from the other, cocoa powder (See *Chocolate Everyday*).
The last step, but not the least : the *conching* This process, which owes its name to the vats that hold the chocolate, was introduced by the Swiss Rodolphe Lindt in 1879. The principle is relatively simple : the paste is kneaded for several hours in order to make it finer and smoother. Conching also allows any final traces of acidity to be removed. Finally, the longer it lasts (usually from 12 to 72 hours), the less bitterness that is present.

Kneading of the chocolate

All that remains is for the chocolate maker to work the chocolate as it cools. They can then give it the shape they wish, or use it for moulding or covering.

Types of Chocolate

Dark chocolate

Dark chocolate must contain a minimum of 43% cocoa to have the right to this appellation. Faced with the recent mania among customers for chocolates rich in cocoa, makers often offer a full array of different percentages of cocoa, and no longer content themselves with a single "dark" offering.

This is how we came to have, from Nestlé, the *Ba·lovento*, *Sumatera* and *Gagnoa*, issued from different varieties of cocoa, the famous *Noir de Noir* (70%) from *Côte d'Or* or even the *Lindt Extra Noir* at 80% cocoa.

Beware, however, since high levels of cocoa are not always a guarantee of quality. One unfortunately finds too often beans that are too acidic or with an incorrect roasting when the level of cocoa reaches or passes 70%. A last point : dark chocolate should ideally have a deep mahogany colour and offer some hints of red. We can then easily avoid a common misconception and replace it with the fact that quality is above all a question of provenance, therefore the type of bean.

As for the "chocoholics" who simply can't be satisfied except by chocolate super charged with cocoa, certain professionals consider this snobbism, if not an outright fault in taste. But, if

www.marmotte.net

there are those who must persist in this arena, know that *Montignac* (creator of the diets of the same name) proposes among others a "chocolate" containing 99% cocoa. It is available from the diet shops. Keep out of the reach of children... !

Milk chocolate

The most consumed type of chocolate worldwide owes its creation to Henri Nestlé who introduced condensed milk. A little later, in 1875, the Swiss Daniel Peter created the first milk chocolate bar. It remains to this day one of the principle Swiss specialties under such brands as *Toblerone* or *Milka*.

To have rights to its name, milk chocolate must contain a minimum of 35% dry extract of cocoa. As for dark chocolate, more and more makers offer a "milk" made from scratch with beans of noble origin. In no specific order, we site *Valrhona* in France, *Nestlé* in Switzerland or *Jacques* in Belgium.

In the same manner as for the previous type, we note its colour, which ideally should have an ochre tint. As for the flavour, it is sad to note that many milk chocolates are too sugary and pasty in the mouth.

Finally, how could we talk about milk chocolate without bringing up the famous psychedelic cow from *Milka* : its mauve and white coat is known all over the world and the friendly bovine has really become a phenomenon. Recently, it has been joined by a cute little marmot who "*puts the chocolate in the aluminium foil...*" An internet site, called simply *www.marmotte.net*, has even been devoted to it by an admirer. A chance to replay the famous ad ....

White chocolate

Numerous chocolate amateurs denounce white chocolate – worse, some chocolate makers won't even make it – under the pretext that it's not really chocolate. It's true that it contains not one centigram of dry cocoa extract, but one of its main ingredients is cocoa butter, without which it wouldn't exist. Forget for a moment that useless state of the purist and savour white chocolate for what it is.

Like other forms of chocolate, it must conform to certain standards : 20% cocoa butter, 14% dry milk solids and 55% sugar. What's more, it is (or was ...) subject to the same norms of production, i.e. that it can not (couldn't) contain anything but products derived from milk or cocoa.

Finally, don't forget that the Swiss have largely specialized in this niche market by offering a good number of products of this type, including the famous *Galak* bars, natural or with puffed rice.

On the other hand, to add fuel to the opinion of its detractors, note that even so, the results of efforts to make white chocolate vary widely ... something that signifies one finds more poor chocolate in "white" then in the other categories : too sugary or too crumbly are the faults most often found.

Filled chocolate

Whether it's white, dark or milk, in bars or tablets, filled chocolate represents a large part of total chocolate production. Certain fillings are grand classics, like *praliné*, hazelnut (whole or pieces), caramel or certain fruit jellies.

Chocolate makers have recourse to the same methods of production as are used for making pralines : *trempage* (soaking or dipping) and *moulage* (moulding). And the analogy with sweets doesn't stop there, because certain makers (*Galler* and *Baptista*, notably) offer bars of filled chocolate divided into four large morsels that they nickname "bar of pralines". Their weight (70g or 2.5oz), the quality of their filling and the numerous varieties contribute to the confusion.

Chocolate de couverture

Although in times past the small and medium sized chocolate makers transformed their cocoa themselves in order to make their finished products, those days seem to be passing away. A few enterprises have

Delivery of the cover chocolate.

Fabrication du praliné.

Praline manufacturing.

specialised in what is called *chocolat de couverture*, that is to say a semi-finished product destined as much for bakeries, biscuit makers and other food artisans or food industries, as for a good number of chocolate makers themselves. Often this means a chocolate high in cocoa butter, more refined in taste and less sugary than the product destined for consumption. From a legal point of view, it must contain a minimum of 31% oils and white chocolate may never carry the appellation *couverture*.

The specialists produce the chocolate according to recipes unique to each client, being a sort of specialised sub-contractor. So, the makers of chocolate *de couverture* use many hundreds of different recipes, according to the whims of their clients. Most of the time, it is delivered to them in liquid form, in tanker trucks.

Among the major makers, we find notably *Barry Callebaut* (world leader since the merger of *Cocoa Barry* with *Callebaut*) in France and in Belgium, *Jacques* in Belgium and *Valrhona* in France. Note also that chocolate *de couverture*, logically enough, is the form of chocolate most produced in the world.

Finally, an amusing anecdote to close : the English term *covering*, as it is used for chocolate, corresponds to a coating of deplorable quality ... it is best not to confuse the terms !!

Storage

Chocolate, like all foodstuffs, has a limited lifespan. To maximize its lifespan, it is wise to follow certain rules :

chocolate cannot withstand heat, see that it is kept at a temperature from 59°F to 64°F ...

chocolate cannot withstand humidity, see that your tablets and bars are kept in a dry area...

chocolate cannot withstand air and light, see that it is kept in a hermetically sealed environment...

chocolate cannot withstand aging, see that it is consumed shortly after opening...

chocolate cannot withstand variations of temperature, see that it is kept in an environment with a constant temperature...

A little pompous, don't you think ? That's our opinion too, and also that of someone who is a real specialist : Jean Galler. *"If you maintained these conditions, the conservation of your chocolate would be perfect and there would be no need to put it in the refrigerator. But who has, in their home, a space that conforms to all these conditions ? So, it is better to put your chocolate in the refrigerator, in a box (...), and take the box out twenty minutes before eating (...), the chocolate will attain its ideal temperature. If you haven't got the patience to wait that long, you would be eating it a little too cold, with the consequence of diminished aroma. But does one eat chocolate to squeeze out the maximum aroma in each mouthful, or rather purely for the pleasure ?"*

The least we can say is that Jean Galler has poked some holes in an old theory, casting a shadow over the commentaries of certain pseudo purists and elitists. Because chocolate is and must remain a pleasure for any moment, a stolen minute on break, a sudden craving between meals, a bar that satisfies on the train, on foot or in the car. We can also reflect this idea back onto other foodstuffs, similar in their philosophy. Haven't you ever sipped a little local rosé without questioning it ? Do you systematically analyse the way in which you are served your cold pint ? So it should be with chocolate...

Whichever type it might be, know that just the same, a chocolate subjected to humidity, or too great a fluctuation in temperature, will rapidly degrade. White traces will appear : this is sugar that is "freed" due to the loss of homogeneity among the oils in the mixture. This situation often leads to a loss of flavour just as chocolate exposed too long to light oxidizes easily and takes on a rancid taste.

Tasting

What a transition, we are finally here ! For the chocolate that was "appreciated" so voraciously since tender infancy can also, once adulthood is reached, become the object of different attentions. We don't mean those famous " chocomaniacs" that are kind of the "alcoholics of chocolate", but the many among us that take the time to understand the messages that the chocolate carries. Because as it is for wine, cognac, beer or even cigars, there are a certain number of codified parameters that unlock the "comprehension" of chocolate.
The goal here is not an in depth study of chocolate tasting criteria. There are more and more specialised books on that level and, generally they are well executed. But, nonetheless, one should know that chocolate uses a series of terms in this arena that are specific to itself,

or borrowed from other domains more habituated to this sort of "literature".

A precise and adapted vocabulary

For example, there is talk of « *crus* » (specific appellations), one evokes the body, the bouquet or the lingering in the mouth as if it were a grand wine. We could also linger over its texture like the amateurs of Havanas or a specialist analysing the head on a beer. The truly impassioned also muse over the consistency by observing and ... listening to the way it breaks, for example. Deeper yet, we can see that the processes of tasting require the use of all five senses (sight, smell,...) to which we add retro-nasal function.

Finally, don't forget that any "tasting" worthy of that name should begin before all else with the reading of the label (isn't it the same for wine, cheese or whisky ?) and that this tasting must always be done under optimal conditions for holding and *hearing* the chocolate.

But knowing the basis for tasting can also reveal poor chocolate. For instance, a chocolate of inferior quality can be easily recognized by the fact that it clings to the palate and takes on a pasty texture when melting in the mouth. It may also provoke a sensation of thirst if it is over sugared.

Better understanding is above all better appreciation

Whatever the type, we can distinguish two methods for tasting chocolate, according to the form it is in.

To whit, filled chocolate and pralines must be bitten since the aromas are enclosed in the chocolate covering and the incision by the teeth frees them. On the other hand, chocolate with incorporated nuts, etc., must melt in the mouth. The next technique is to press it with the tongue against the palate and thereby impregnate the taste buds in order to appreciate the subtleties it conceals.

But once again, it would be useless to abandon the simple pleasure of munching a piece of chocolate on the run by systematically overburdening oneself with overly ceremonious principles ... not to say that it isn't agreeable to learn how to understand chocolate and discover the minutiae of these creations that had been hidden.

The pralines

A little history

The definition of a *praline* differs depending on the country of origin. In France and Switzerland, it remains in conformity with the original recipe, invented by accident by the Duke of Plessis-Praslin's cook : a roasted almond, bathed in a sugar syrup and chilled. It contains no chocolate then, and seems to belong more to what the Belgians call *dragée* (sugar almond). In 1912 the Belgian chocolate maker Jean Neuhaus gave it another definition : a roasted almond or hazel nut, covered with chocolate. Faced with its popularity among the people, other versions followed rapidly and the demand was so high that a special package had to be created to transport, and of course serve, them : in 1915 the *ballotin* was born.

But in the history of cocoa, the praline is, above all else, the pinnacle of chocolate *de luxe*, something we consume to excite the taste buds for a few moments of ephemeral happiness.

Today, Belgian pralines have contributed a great deal to the country's recognition as a specialist in chocolate. And just as each chocolate maker, confectioner and baker often has their own recipes (*Leonidas* offers an array of more than 80 varieties), there are some grand classics that everyone, artisan or industrial, should offer.

Appellation d'origine contrôlée

Belgian pralines, in such high demand from tourists who visit Brussels, Bruges or Ghent, are of course exported to the four corners of the world and are always greatly appreciated. *Neuhaus*, and also *Godiva*, *Leonidas* and *Guylian*, just to name a few, are known all over the world and are usually sold through specific boutiques. On that same topic, the *skyshops* at Brussels-National Airport and elsewhere are a large part of these resellers.

As for the "generalist" producers like *Côte d'Or*, they often make their own assortment of pralines, even though they don't have the same attraction as the specialty makers'. Purists agree, arguing that a praline must be a fresh product, served from its golden carton and sold by weight.

Finally, take note that the French and the Swiss market chocolate specialties, in addition to Belgian pralines, which are similar in form and spirit, but carry the simple moniker "chocolates".

How are pralines made ?

Two techniques allow the building of a praline : *moulage* (moulding) and *enrobage* (coating). The first is, at its origin, more specifically Belgian, while the second is more the style of France or Switzerland.

Moulding consists of, as its name indicates, pouring chocolate into a mould. After cooling and hardening, the maker applies the filling, which he covers with another layer of liquid chocolate. After hardening again, the pralines are un-moulded and turned over.

Coating is a more modern technique. It consists of simply plunging the garnish into a bath of liquid chocolate, or passing it

Making of traditional pralines.

under a "curtain" of chocolate, after arranging the fillings on a moving belt. For designs using chocolate of other colours, the praline also receives an additional "*giclée*" (squirt). Next the confections pass through a cooling tunnel, which allows them to solidify.
The decoration is another important step. Here, each maker can let their imagination run wild in order to differentiate themselves from their competitors. Anything is possible : particular shapes, hazelnut or other nut meats, grains or folds of chocolate...
As for the thickness of the coating chocolate or shell, it should be as thin as possible, crisp to the tooth, and never hide the perfumes exhaled by the filling. It should come into play only as a part of the whole, while melting over the tongue, developing a unique flavour born of the association of the chocolate and its garnish.

The principle varieties

Although many praline makers offer a wide variety, and still others are braver than most in daring certain combinations that are more or less unusual, there are certain unavoidable examples that each artisan must offer. Here is a glimpse, keeping in mind that most of these "classics" can exist in three variations : white, dark and milk chocolate.

Crème fraîche

Flavoured or not, crème fraîche serves as the base for many pralines made with the *moulage* technique. They are relatively rare as they are difficult to execute ... and even

Chocolate and statistics

England is the most profitable country for the chocolate industry since it spends 5.4 million dollars per year on chocolate.

The regular chocolate consumers (more or less 6 pounds a week) can expect to live one year more than those who don't eat chocolate at all.

Cocoa is the third worldwide most exported foodstuff after sugar and coffee.

45 different countries, spread out between the tropic of Cancer and the tropic of Capricorn, cultivate cocoa.

80% of the chocolate production is carried out in Europe and North America.

more difficult to keep properly fresh. Sugar and sometimes butter are often added. It isn't uncommon to find cocoa as well.

Ganache

Is it better to be taken for a *ganache* or an *imbecile* ? Hard to say, since the first term, though it seems more elegant, is a typically Parisian synonym for the second. In any case, this is how a XIXth century pastry chef scolded his apprentice for a "monumental" goof. He had just let boiling milk spill onto several tablets of chocolate, at the same time giving birth to one of the most popular praline fillings.

The original recipe has been improved of course. Today it is boiled cream, with the addition of twice its weight in chocolate. Butter is most often used as the binding agent, and of course sugar.

With this as a base, chocolate makers can let their overflow-

ing imaginations run wild. We can define classic ganaches, but also others infused with coffee, fruit extracts (raspberry), spices (vanilla or saffron), or aromatic plants (mint, basil or...fennel). The cream takes on beautiful colours. The famous owner of *La Maison du Chocolat*, the Basque Robert Linxe, revealed that he let himself be tempted by the desire to elaborate a ganache with ... tobacco.

A similar technique is used to make *crème au beurre* (butter cream), a mix of sugar and butter, beaten while cold. Coffee is sometimes added (mocha cream) or liqueur.

Gianduja

Gianduja is a mix of equal parts, toasted and crushed hazelnuts, sugar, cocoa butter and milk chocolate *de couverture* Sometimes the paste also contains almonds or other nuts. Invented in 1851 by Isidore Caffarel, son of the founder of a famous Italian chocolate maker, it owes its name to one of the heroes of that country's unification. It is often presented in the shape of small ingots wrapped in gold paper.

Liqueurs

Pralines filled with liqueurs use a different technique than is used for the other varieties. Between the chocolate and the alcohol, the praline contains a thin layer of crystallized sugar with a touch of starch. It is, in fact, an envelope to hold the liquid, making the coating easier.

There are also kirsch pralines, in the centre of which is found a macerated cherry : the best

known example is of course the *Mon Cheri* from *Ferrero*.

In a box, they are easily identified thanks to their coloured aluminium wrappers.

Manon

This is more a kind of praline than a filling in particular. Besides, several varieties exist since there is no official recipe. A Manon is, first of all, larger than the average praline, filled with crème fraîche or butter cream (sometimes infused with coffee) and covered with white chocolate or hard sugar. Some are decorated with a hazelnut or other nutmeat. They are often round in shape, although rectangular Manons are found more and more.

As for the origin of the name, it is as mysterious as the inventor. However, two Belgian chocolate makers have rendered them the highest honour by dedicating their signboards to them : *Le Chocolatier Manon* in

The *ballotin*, specially designed for pralines.

Brussels and the *Chocolaterie aux Manons* in Quiévrain.

Marzipan

Marzipan is not truly a praline if it is presented alone, without either cocoa or cocoa butter. But, this mixture of sugar and almonds (30 to 60%) often serves as a base for building chocolate fillings. It is covered using the coating technique.

Praliné

It is evidently not a coincidence that *praliné* and *praline* share the same root. *Praliné* is in fact a mixture of ground hazelnuts or almonds, often toasted, to which is added caramelised sugar. The ideal proportions are one part dried nutmeats for one part sugar. The pieces of nut should ideally be just perceptible on the tongue and the palate.

Truffé

This interior, which obviously draws its name from the chocolate truffle, another gourmet chocolate treat, is a mixture of chocolate, sugar and butter, to which is often added a few drop of liqueur. A deep, almost black, brown, this filling is a little denser than those made from a cream base.

Presentation and storage

For an amateur chocolate lover, what is more beautiful to behold than the display case at a chocolate boutique ? This is one aspect of things that the seller cannot overlook, since, especially in this domain, the consumers devour first with their eyes, before calmly savouring these sweets.

Then, after the eternal dilemma of choosing – since a choice must be made – the pralines are sealed in a box (the famous *ballotin*) designed to protect them as much from the voyage and light...as from the eyes of those you pass who might be jealous of your new acquisition. On this point, *Leonidas* must certainly be the most concerned for their customer's future because their golden cartons are regularly wrapped in three successive layers...!

In the store, pralines are kept in a refrigerated case, holding the temperature at 15°C. The household refrigerator, though it maintains a lower temperature, is also the best environment for keeping chocolate at home. Not that the chocolate really requires it (see *Chocolate, Storage*), but rather it is clearly preferable to maintain the freshness of the fillings, especially when they contain cream or butter. Ideally, the pralines should be taken out 10 to 15 minutes before the start of the tasting.

As for the duration of storage for fresh pralines, it is advised not to go over 8 or 10 days from the date of purchase. Pre-packaged pralines (*Guylian, Duc d'O,...*) of course have an expiration date, printed on their packaging. They may last for several months.

Finally, don't forget that pralines are, and have been since the date of their invention, one of the most prized gifts (to offer others, or yourself).

Three giants of chocolate

France
Belgium
Switzerland

Beginnings in common

In Europe and, dare we say the world, Belgium and also France and Switzerland, are the three principal producers of quality chocolate. Although their approach to the product differs somewhat today, their beginnings show some interdependencies.

We have already seen how cocoa made its entry into France, via the angle of royal marriages between the ruling families of France and Spain. The latter occupied the Netherlands at the time when cocoa was introduced into Europe, and so it was only natural that we would find chocolate among the favourite beverages in the salons of a region not yet named Belgium. As for Switzerland, they joined the cause of chocolate after the mayor of Zurich, Heinrich Escher, visited Brussels one fine day in 1697. That is unless it happened thanks to merchants arriving from Italy...

But, each country also has a personal history...

Selected vintages of French chocolate

France

Of course, *France* profited from its commercial relationships with its colonies (Martinique, Guyana and Guadeloupe for example) where cocoa was cultivated. This situation allowed them a supply without a middleman. >From the XVIIth century on, chocolate makers therefore became more numerous and more experimental.

In comparison to its two neighbours, France offers a chocolate of slightly lower quality on average. However, we find in France some producers with exceptional quality (*Linxe*, *Dufoux*, *Valrhona*, *Weiss*, *Bernachon*,...) but unfortunately too small scale, especially outside of its own borders. As a general rule, there is good chocolate produced there ... but at a fairly high price. To illustrate this point, note that an honours list of the best chocolate makers in the world was recently compiled. Of the 35 selected, there were only 15 to gain the maximum (3 stars) and among them we find...8 French.

The *bleu-blanc-rouge* makers are generally very creative. But on that front, there are two opposing schools. One group of chocolate makers offer very traditional products, without eccentricities. At the same time, many of their competitors put chocolate “into every sauce”, if we can use the phrase. In this category, we find the worst and the best : absurd creations and others very popular, useless innovations and milestones, fleeting entries and new standards.

If France had to be associated with one type of chocolate, it would surely be dark chocolate, high in cocoa (+55%).

Belgium

Contrary to what one might imagine, *Belgium* did not specialise in chocolate due to the cocoa being grown in its future colonies because it wasn't grown on the "dark continent" until the XIXth century. However, neither can we deny that this situation was a determining factor in the development of the chocolate industry.

Belgium is the country of variety and also a certain creativity. Homeland of the *praline*, it is also one of the multitude of flavours that have become classics. As in France, the...standards are high when it comes to quality and Belgian chocolate makers often offer an excellent ratio of price to quality.

Many makers have export channels, both via their own brand names (*Leonidas*, *Godiva*, *Neuhaus*,...), and thanks to specialised re-sellers. Also, we find even on the supermarket shelves the labels of the

The Royal Greenhouse of Laeken (Brussels) made of chocolate, created by Corné Port-Royal.

1
CACAO
ZACK

huge multinationals (*Côte d'Or* and *Callebaut* above all).
Belgium would be associated with filled chocolate and, in a general sense, lightly sweeter chocolate than its homologue from France.

Switzerland

The reputation of the ***Swiss*** in matters of chocolate needs no description. It is often qualified as smooth, sweet and milky and in the four corners of the globe, Swiss chocolate enjoys an aura of incomparability. Even so, of the multitude of chocolate makers to whom the country is home, very few are known outside. Switzerland has many artisans that make chocolate that melds together tradition and quality. Unfortunately, with scarce exception, most of them do not export and the fruits of their labour never make it outside the county's borders except through the "*free shops*" at the airport and internet sales.

The Swiss Cailler, who modernized the grinding techniques

On the other hand, Switzerland is most assuredly the number one industrial producer of quality chocolate. It must be said that most of the inventions that revolutionized the sector were

Chocolate workshop in the Thirties.

due to Swiss citizens. To whit we cite the invention of F.-L. Cailler who introduced a new method of grinding. A little time later, in 1830, his compatriot Kohler created the first tablet with hazelnuts. In 1875 Peter used a Nestlé invention (condensed milk) to make the first milk chocolate. Finally, Rodolphe Lindt perfected the process in 1879 by developing conching, a process serving to diminish the bitterness and humidity of the cocoa.

Swiss advertisement for soluble cocoa (1890).

Inventions that mark an era

Today, the largest are named *Nestlé*, *Toblerone*, *Milka*, *Suchard* and *Lindt* but only a few multinationals share the shelf space in the supermarkets of the western countries.

Nestlé has factories all over the world and is active in most of the agro-alimentary business sectors. The purchase of the English concern *Rowntree* (*Smarties*, *After Eight*, *Lion*, *Kit Kat*,...) at the end of the eighties made it the universal leader in chocolate.

The internal competition consists primarily of a four-headed empire, poetically named *Kraft-Jacobs-Suchard-Côte d'Or* (itself falling under the direction of the American group *Philip Morris*).

Lastly, without wanting to harp on the subject, note none the less that the Swiss decided not to follow the other dissidents of the European Union, namely France and Belgium. On this front, though the recipes remain unchanged for the interior market, it is not uncommon to find vegetable oils and powdered skim milk in products destined for exportation. A sad path to profitability...mitigated by the fact that the Swiss only authorize a maximum of 2% vegetable fats !

Finally, Switzerland would obviously be called the country of milk chocolate and white chocolate.

Chocolate makers

BAPTISTA

Chaussée de Nivelles, 52
1461 Ittre
Tel. 02 366 02 69
Fax 02 366 35 39
e-mail :
info@chocolat-baptista.com
http://www.chocolat-baptista.com
Year founded: 1984
Export : 70% of production
Distribution : retailers, grocers

The Selection

Outside of a small array of tablets, last born to the family but nonetheless classics, Baptista enchants with their famous "*pralines en bâton*" or "praline bar". These bars of a relatively outdated size (70g or 2.47oz) are available in regular flavours (Red Fruit, Pear-Banana,...) or more unique flavours (*Manon*, dark/white marble, white/milk marble,...). The other specialty of the house, the pralines, continue to do well despite the 27 varieties only appearing at retailers during the holiday season.

History

Marc Baptista is a computer scientist by training. He started his career at the beginning of the 70's at Philips, up until the day when one of the PME that he serviced decided to hire him. They were specialists in dairy products, which allowed our man to familiarize himself with the sector and, in his turn, to create his own distribution company in 1979.

But he quickly realized that it was better to lead the production of a single product and he turned his attention to chocolate. In 1984, Marc Baptista founded a company to which he

gave his name and installed himself in Brussels.

An initial investment of 1.7 million BEF permitted the launch of an essentially manual operation. The enterprise started with the production of pralines, but given the seasonal nature of the product, they undertook the making of chocolate bars. However, the basic recipes weren't changed, and thus " *pralines en batons* " appeared.

Giving a high priority to the freshness and quality of his products, Marc Baptista wanted nonetheless to make his enterprise more productive, and thereby more successful. To that end, in 1992 he invested in the construction of a gigantic 17,200 ft² building in Ittre, in

The Callebaut factory in the past.

the Belgian Province of Walloon Brabant. At the same time, he mechanised that location to provide a total production of around 4 tonnes per day, under the watchful eye of 6 to 8 people, according to the season.

Today, the workflow remains the same, something that signifies they adapted the tools of production to the recipes, and not the inverse as is too often the case. In comparison, we can see that Baptista produced just 10 tonnes annually back in 1987 and employed only 4 people. As for today's goals, they are split between those for Belgium (increase their presence in non-specialty stores) and those for export (diversify and increase the number of countries where they are present). The chocolate maker also hopes to conform to ISO 9002 criteria very soon.

Just between us...

One of the other objectives confided in us is the growth of their " Private Label " creation. This is their production of chocolate products for other name brands more widely known to the public. Did you know, for example, that *Baptista* makes a chocolate for *Decathlon* and another for *Biotherm* ?

BARRY CALLEBAUT

Aalstersestraat,122
9280 Wieze
Tel. 053 73 02 11
Fax 053 78 04 63
http://www.callebaut.be
Year founded: 1911
Export : 70 % of production.
Distribution : large distribution of finished products, venture to transform chocolate into *chocolat de couverture* (for other chocolate makers, biscuit makers, bakeries,...)

The Selection

For the average consumer, *Callebaut* offers a classic array of tablets and bars, among which one finds a few originals : Vanilla-Raspberry, Strawberry or *Panaché* (orange-rum raisin). Directed at home bakers, the *Choc' Idée* are decorations and small chocolate dishes, and the *Callets Desserts* help make an easy chocolate fondue. For gourmet breakfasts, the *Matinettes* revive the true *tartine au chocolat*. Among the other " niche " products, we would also point out the tablets of *Extra Amer* (Bitter) 62% chocolate and other organic agriculture products.
Finally, despite the majority of its activities being directed toward the professional sector, *Callebaut* still has a bright future on the supermarket shelves.

History

Few amateurs of chocolate know it, but *Callebaut* was before everything else ...a brewery ! Eugène Callebaut indeed founded what was an industrial brewery named *De Ploeg* (*The Plough*) in 1845. A few years later he added a malting house,

A scrumptious chocolate bar that you can munch just as it comes or savour in a delicious chocolate dessert. Only real Belgian chocolate made from 100% cocoa butter and using the best traditional methods will do.

Nothing can beat the real thing.

a dairy and a flourmill. Next came the production of mineral water and soft drinks. His two sons, Clément and Charles-Louis soon took up the reins.
In the early years of the XXth century the company was baptised *Gebroeders Callebaut.* At that time, a chocolate division was created to balance the seasonal nature of brewing. The two functions remained closely tied though, since Octaaf and Richard Callebaut shared the responsibilities... and the personnel.
The production of coating chocolate *(chocolat de couverture)* began in 1925, while in 1930 two distinct companies were born, separating the brewing activities from the chocolate making. As for the other divisions of the company, they faded away one after the other.

Beneficial reorganizations

The development of exports and an increasingly diverse array of products allowed *Callebaut* to gain a favourable reputation outside the borders of Belgium and even Europe by 1965. The situation stabilised like this until 1979, the year when *Alken* purchased the *Callebaut* brewery. In 1981, *Interfood*, a Swiss foodstuffs company, joined the dance as a majority stakeholder in the *Chocolaterie Callebaut.* The alliance could have broken through to a new level. But, two years later, *Klaus Jacobs*, another Swiss multinational, took over *Interfood.* The enterprise owned a series of factories all over the world and was also the majority owner of *Van Houten*, chocolate maker from the Netherlands specialising in cocoa powder.
A new drama in 1990, when *Klaus Jacobs* sold *Jacobs Suchard* to *Philip Morris*...who sold back *Callebaut* in the exchange (are you following this... ?). By contract, the American giant was authorized to market Wieze chocolates until 1995 : a famous paradox if you know that *Philip Morris* was already the owner of...*Côte d'Or* !
The story didn't stop there, because in 1996 the two largest European coating chocolate specialists joined one another to form *Barry Callebaut.* The new company, after passing the review of the fair competition commission, thus became the world leader in this specialty.

Chocolate is good business

Today, the group markets cocoa products under five different brands : *Cocoa Barry* (France), *Callebaut* (Belgium), *Carma* (Switzerland), *Bensdorp* and *Van Houten* (the Netherlands). They are spread among 23 production sites all over the world and are therefore always close to their clients. The Wieze factory produces 188,000 tonnes of chocolate per year while the total for the group is the incredible number of 555,000 tonnes annually. Along the same lines, *Barry Callebaut*'s cocoa bean purchases come to more than 12% of the world's total production...and not one bean less!

The Franco-Belgian branch is a veritable " data bank " for bakers, pastry makers, chocolate makers and restaurateurs. *Barry Callebaut* offers no less than 1800 recipes to its clients. Of course, it isn't so much for different flavours, but for variations on such parameters as bitterness, sugar or viscosity. Often, these recipes are developed in collaboration with the clients themselves, something that means each client can make use of products tailored to their wants and needs. In fact, we could call *Barry Callebaut* the " keeper of chocolate secrets ".

Defender of quality chocolate, *Barry Callebaut* maintains a presence in Africa to watch over the beans destined for export. To the same end, they have seven research centres that allow them to introduce new products, and to improve those that are already marketed. These centres themselves work with Universities and private laboratories.

At *Callebaut*, the customer is king, whether large or small. All their information is at the client's disposal, for their benefit. Finally, the young companies just starting out in the world of cocoa can also count on their support. They make available to them all the information possible from the legal and commercial level.

Just between us...

In 1990, *Callebaut* received the universal certification of quality ISO 9002. It was the first Belgian foodstuff company to receive this and the first chocolate maker in the world. Today, *Barry Callebaut* has reached the next level by securing ISO 9001 certification.

Old advertisement.

A closer look at...

...the specialist products. *Barry Callebaut* offers products adapted towards an ever growing clientele. To whit, several niche markets have seen the light of day such as :

- a complete line for diabetics (chocolate, nut pastes, fillings,...), using fructose, lactose, maltose or polydextrose ;

- chocolates and other products using.kosher nuts, destined for Jewish communities ;

- *fairtrade* products, which respect agricultural efforts in developing countries ;

- chocolate whose ingredients are at a minimum 95% organic, certified and controlled with the assistance of the European Union. In this category we find the *BIO Fondant* (melting) and *au lait* (milk chocolate) tablets made from beans *d'origine* – that is to say from a single source (Java, Saõ Tome or Grenada).

BRUYERRE

rue François-Léon Bruyerre
6041 Gosselies (Charleroi)
Tel. 071 85 22 42
Fax 071 85 33 38
e-mail : bruyerre@interweb.be
http://www.bruyerre.be
Year founded: 1909
Export : on sale in Paris, Cologne, New York, London, Tokyo
Distribution : branches in Gosselies, Brussels, Namur and in many bakeries

The Selection

Made from cream, ganache or even gianduja, the pralines from *Chocolatier Bruyerre* are simply excellent, and no connoisseur would pretend otherwise. Poetically nicknamed, they sweep the amateur from the classic Manon (in 5 ! varieties) to the eccentric *Cannelle* (cinnamon), on to the romantic *Amourette* and *Valentine*, finally to the very chic *Argenteuil* and *Amboise*. The home county wasn't forgotten either, with the *Iris* (nicknamed the *Charleroi Praline*) and of course the *Saveur de Vallée* (with real citrus from Spain !). Finally, the *Liqueur Selection* is blessed with a unique praline incorporating Ricard.

History

Ninety-two years ! That's an age that definitely qualifies as respectable, for the *Chocolaterie Bruyerre* founded in 1909. But the time for retirement is nowhere near and the venerable old lady has no doubt never felt quite so spry.

François-Léon Bruyerre embarked on his commercial activities by selling what were called " colonial goods " (dried fruits, vanilla, sugar,...). A few years later, in 1922, he broke camp and installed himself in an old biscuit factory, situated on a street called Faubourg de Bruxelles in Gosselies. The company is still there today. He then struck out into the production of pralines, chocolate bars, confections and products destined for baker-pastry chefs. Growth continued and the chocolate maker prospered...until 1940, when the Second World War broke out. Business collapsed and the company was in danger of going under throughout the five years of conflict. But just as the conflict found an end, François-Léon Bruyerre passed away.

His two sons-in-law, Emile and Maurice Collet, took over control of operations, and profited from the economic re-birth to develop a new product line : materials for bakeries (mixers, mechanical kneaders, refrigerators and freezers, bread cutting machines,...). In this arena, Bruyerre was truly a trailblazer in a country that was still healing its wounds. As for ingredients, it was also a time of diversification. And so, those same bakers could avail themselves of confectionary products and materials for making pastries : pudding, chocolate, fruit compotes, jams,... On the other hand, the *chocolat* division was re-centred solely production of pralines, relegating the production of tablets to the history books. More than an economic reason, it was really more of a choice, at a time when larger chocolate makers where developing.

Four divisions toward a common goal

The sixties were a time to follow a course of expansion. Another division was born, centred around the production of furnishings for stores (display cases, counters,...) and the distribution outlet grew considerably with re-sellers throughout the Walloon region, in Limbourg and also in the Grand Duchy of Luxembourg.

The next decade was, as in most cases, not nearly as robust. But, despite the disappearance of certain praline fillings, the effects of the economic crisis were fairly limited. At the same time, the third generation took up the reins of the company and dove into development of the furniture division. At the dawn of the eighties, *Bruyerre* was becoming a public company.

The enterprise had a breath of fresh air in 1984 when it became the *Bruyère Group*. Thus, the different divisions of the company took the names *Belgram Equipment* (production materials, store fixtures,...), *Bruyerre* (primary materials, packaging, frozen products,...), *Bruyerre Fournitout* (smaller materials, decorations,...) and of course *Le Chocolatier Bruyerre*, the chocolate maker, which moved a few hundred yards away.

Today, each part of the group rides atop its domain and together they have probably never been so dynamic. A promising state for a company that prides itself on being among the oldest bakery-pastry suppliers in the Belgium.

Just between us...

Did you know that *Bruyerre* has new plans for expansion ? We must still speak of it in the future tense at the time these lines are being written. But if the time-table holds true, the chocolate division will shift activities in March 2001 to a brand new building, no doubt more fitted to modern production. Those sensitive to the old ways can take heart : its not a question of moving the tools from one region to another for fiscal reasons, Gosselies remains the neurological centre of the brand !

A closer look at...

...the Manons. As we have said, (see the chapter *Pralines*), Manons are a whole category of pralines, rather than a specific type. Here then are some very intriguing examples.

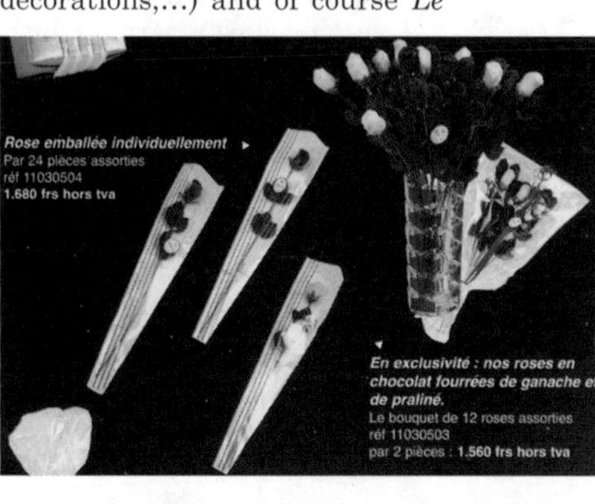

Bruyerre offers 5 pra-lines falling into the Manon category :

Manon Café : a *praliné* base and mo-cha crème fraîche ar coated in white choc-olate. It is decorate with a chocolate cov-ered coffee bean.

Manon Chocolat identical to the pre

ceding, but decorated with chocolate sprinkles.

Manon Crème Fraîche : the most classic, made with vanilla crème fraîche and a *praliné* base, coated with white chocolate striped with dark chocolate.

Manon Dame Blanche : almost the exact inverse of the preceding, a coating of dark chocolate striped with white chocolate, inside there is crème fraîche on a *praliné* base.

Manon Coco : assuredly the most exotic of the bunch. The coating of dark chocolate sprinkled with coconut shavings, covers a *praliné* filling and...coconut crème fraîche.

CAFÉ-TASSE

Avenue Reine Astrid, 1
1440 Wauthier-Braine
Tel. 02 366 96 14
Fax 02 366 90 32
e-mail : cafetasse@skynet.be
http://www.cafe-tasse.com
http://www.cafe-tasse.be
Year founded: 1988
Export : in 30 countries around Europe and the world
Distribution : Café-Tasse Store (Brussels and...Shanghai), approved agents, cafés, restaurants, ...

The Selection

Nothing but the most delicious weets to accompany a nice deep lack cup ! Although the flagship roduct is the *napolitain* (inused itself, therefore without lling), there is a rich and varied rray offered by this little comany in the Brabant. We point ut in particular the tablets of *Noir Cannelle* (Dark Cinnamon), *Noir Orange* (Dark Ornge), *Noir Menthe* (Dark Mint) nd *Noir Thé* (Dark Tea) as well as a complete assortment of chocolates at 77% cocoa.

For mixing into milk, *Café-Tasse* also offers different varieties of cocoa powder, infused with orange, coconut or even honey. Finally, to permit the full appreciation of the relationship between coffee and chocolate, the line-up includes the famous *Santos*, chocolate covered coffee beans.

History

To understand the origins of *Café-Tasse* we must roll back the clock ... three centuries ! In fact, it was in the XVIIth century in Paris that a certain Procope imagined devoting a site to the consumption of coffee, an exotic and modern beverage. To compliment this, Precope decided to add a few sweets, confections and chocolates.

The tradition perpetuated itself, so well in fact that still today most places that serve coffee accompany the black beverage with a little sweet. It was this particular niche that François Decarpentrie wanted to explore when he set out, in 1988, on the grand adventure that is chocolate. But don't imagine that our man was a novice : famous houses such as *Neuhaus* and *Godiva* had earlier welcomed him within their walls.

The " Président-Fondateur ", as the employees call him, added an ecological angle to the product. To whit, the packaging is made exclusively from recycled materials, whether it is paper, wood or jute. Elsewhere, research into customer satisfaction is pushed to the extreme with, notably, the creation of a " Santos " that is decaffeinated.

Just between us...

The *Café-Tasse Store* in Brussels gives customers the chance to buy, in addition to the diverse forms of chocolate, serving pieces for chocolate and coffee in ceramic. The cups are hand-made by Belgian artisans.

A closer look at...

...Coated Dried Fruits. This is with no doubt the most original category of the *Café-Tasse* repertoire. It is composed of 11 varieties of dried fruit, each covered in a delicious chocolate. Among them we find almonds dressed in cocoa powder (like the Périgord nuts), dark chocolate or sugar encrusted and also raisins and Brazil nuts, covered in white chocolate, dark chocolate and milk chocolate, and packaged together. Finally, other assortments are more classic and uniformly covered in either dark or milk chocolate.

CORNÉ PORT ROYAL - VAN PARIJS

Avenue Mercator, 10
Z.I. Wavre-Nord
1300 Wavre
Tel. 010 24 13 66
Fax. 010 24 11 52
http://www.chez.com/corne
Year founded: 1930
Distribution : in the brand's 40 stores

The Selection

Does Princess Mathilde like cinnamon ? Who knows ? In any case, there is a praline with this spice that bears her name. But far from limiting itself to this creation, which is as media conscious as it is royal, *Corné Port-Royal* presents a surprising diversity of flavours, camped out exclusively in the praline category. Many among them are available in more than one type of chocolate (dark, milk or sometimes white) among which we find *Automne* (Autumn - filled with nuts), *Versailles* (chocolate ganache) and even *Zigzag* (gianduja and puffed rice). Finally, take note of the presence of two " authentic " Manons, made with a coating of *fondant* sugar (Vanilla and Coffee).

History

The history started in 1920, when Englebert Vanparijs installed himself in Brussels and began making pralines in the artisan fashion. These immediately started selling in the luxury boutiques and seduced the aristocratic families. Their fabrication was done completely by hand and Englebert himself dreamt up many recipes...most of which are those still in use today.

In 1932, Vanparijs opened his first store on the Boulevard Lemonnier and thereby become one of the pioneers of the chocolate boutique. In the face of the success of his product, Vanparijs purchased a building in Schaerbeek in order to further develop his activities. It is in this building that the *Vanparijs* chocolates were made until the construction of the sole facility in Wavre in 1988.

The years and generations passed, as the mania for chocolate grew and grew. Shortly after the Second World War Robert Vanparijs came to join

his father in the business and a new boutique, situated near the *Bruxelles-Nord* train station, came alongside the first. In 1973, André, grand-son of Englebert Vanparijs, took up his place in the family business.

A more than necessary " *de-localisation* "

In 1985 exportation to the United States began. France and Great Britain fell into step along the same path. This increase in production caused the move to the Province of Walloon Brabant since the Japanese and American demanded modern installations following the latest hygiene standards. And so, the Vanparijs family and their 25 craftsmen moved to Wavre, to a sparkling new factory that matched their ambitions. This was clearly communicated on the 1st of February 1988 with the changing of the company to a *Société Anonyme* and the modification of the trade name to *Vanparys*, doubtless a move to make the denomination more universal.

At the start of the 1990's, *Vanparys* took over the brand *Corné Port-Royal* and its 12 franchise stores. The re-acquisition of this brand, that has existed since 1930 and specialises in Manons, most notably allowed the gamut to be enlarged with the addition of crème fraîche pralines.

Today, in Belgium the group's products are marketed under the name *Corné Port-Royal* while France enjoys *Vanparys* chocolates. The *Corné Port-Royal* boutiques number 28 and are for the most part situated in Brussels and Walloon Brabant. The *Vanparys* stores number 19 today, of which 8 belong to the *Vanparys France* branch.

Corné - Vanparys today employs 50 people and its principle markets are Belgium, France and England. Twice, in 1993 and 1998, the factory in the Brabant had to be enlarged, as the annual production rose to 500 tonnes in 1999. In short, there is no doubt that the dawning third millennium could propel what started out as a little chocolate maker, into a giant in the world of luxury chocolates...

CÔTE D'OR

Brusselsesteenweg, 450
1500
Halle
Tel. 02 362 31 11
Fax 02 356 04 72
http://www.cotedor.com
Year founded: 1883
Export : over 50% of production
Distribution : large and average sized stores, grocers, bakeries, vending machines,...

The Selection

Three pages ! Almost three pages would be needed in order to describe the selection from the most famous Belgian chocolate maker. So, we must linger over a few particulars, something we're sure won't disappoint the sensitive reader that you are. *Côte d'Or*, in the tablet

The logo for the centenary

version, offers two distinct categories : the first fairly classic (though even it has a marzipan and pecan selection) and the second baptised as *Sensation*. A well chosen term, because the feelings these fine tablets provide are truly pleasant. Among these tablets, we would underline the *Noir Orange* (Dark Chocolate Orange) with zest in the chocolate itself and also the *Lait Intense* (Intense Milk) a duo of milk chocolate with a dark chocolate layer on top. Appreciated by the Petit Futé.

Côte d'Or in the bar version proposes an incredible diversity from which we pull the most original : Avocado, Coconut, Almond Nougat and of course the famous *praliné* Dessert 58. Kids being what they are in the sweets isle at the supermarket, *Côte d'Or* also created for them mini-bars named *Codo*.

We often cross paths with *Mignonnettes* (Milk, Fondant, Mocha, *Noir de Noir* or Gianduja) next to a cup of coffee. Never try to take these on a trip in the car, especially in Summer. We tried and they won't survive it, and neither will your luggage!

Côte d'Or, has, in addition, the delicious *Bouchées* shaped like elephants, pre-packaged pralines, a chocolate mousse (with the help of Yoplait), the famous *Chokotoff* that only melts in the mouth, the *Supertoff* and lots of other *(s)toff...*

History

When, on 24th April 1883, the Belgian Charles Neuhaus (imagine that... !?) and the clerk from *the Commercial Court* gave birth to the brand *Côte d'Or*, they were probably far from imagining that one of the most emblematic of Belgium's corporations had just been brought into the world.

But why " Côte d'Or " (Gold Coast) ? Well, don't you find it a name that conjures up dreams and exoticism ? Doesn't it evoke for you irresistible desires for leisure, and pleasure ? This was probably also the perception that Neuhaus had, and so he chose that name, which today's Ghana also sported before its independence and...which is one of the principle world producers of cocoa ! Some say that he was also taken by the beauty of the postage stamps that came from that country.

Nonetheless, six years after he created it, Neuhaus, not seeing his descendents taking up the reins, decided to sell his enterprise to the Bieswal family, from Veurne (Furnes). Shortly after, a certain Lambert Michiels made his appearance. He also installed himself as a chocolate maker, in the portion of the building that Bieswal did not occupy. The two men maintained the relationship of happy neighbours, until 1906, when they decided to associate with one another by creating the *Alimenta* company. It was in this era that the famous elephant appeared, which remains today the symbol *par excellence* of the brand, evoking exoticism, will and force.

The year 1911 marked a turning point, *Alimenta* transformed itself into a cooperative company and the famous yellow and gold packaging appeared. Then, between the two World Wars, *Côte D'Or* set out to conquer the country, with the help of an array of chocolate bars that filled out over the years. Its notoriety didn't reach much further than the region of Brussels at the time, though.

Two Exhibitions are better than one

In 1935, Brussels welcomed for the first time the World's Fair. It was a perfect chance to make oneself known all over the world. To celebrate the event, *Côte D'Or* built a pavilion of " colonial " splendour and created the *Mignonnettes*. Originally meant to be offered only to the exhibition's visitors, these little treats survive even today.

Then, after the Second World War and the healing of the wounds, the future European capital welcomed, again, technology's window to the world. This time, the '58 World's Fair and, there again, *Côte D'Or* took advantage of the event to launch the much appreciated *Dessert 58*. This milk chocolate packed with a delicious and original *praliné* was first launched in the form of a bar before being available in tablets. Like the *Mignonnettes,* it still has a place among the best sellers from *Côte D'Or,* even though it wasn't meant to last this long. Whatever the case, this demonstration of planetary *savoir-faire* allowed *Côte D'Or* to considerably enlarge their " playing field ".

Beginning in the 50's, *Côte D'Or* underwent a true unfurling, via inventions and innovations, notably

in associated sectors. The most famous of these still makes the largest portion of sales in its category : the *Chokotoff.*

Côte d'Or was the sponsor of Eric Tabarly

The era of overflow

Next, in 1987, the then Swiss group *Jacobs Suchard* acquired the brand with the elephant, and many Belgians decried the treason, perhaps a little too fast. It was because many of them considered (as is still true today) *Côte D'Or* as THE chocolate of reference : it was a little like the " yard stick " for Belgium, with qualitative and flavour comparisons often being made against its own. And when the factory on *Bara* street closed its doors in order to move into more modern facilities on the periphery of the city, there were thousands of train passengers that longed for the days when their morning commute to the capital was punctuated with a warm and soft wave of chocolate.

In 1990 *Jacobs Suchard* was integrated with " *an American holding company active in agro-alimentary business* " (who also made cigarettes NOT of chocolate...). This action, followed three years later by a conjoining of *Kraft* into the heart of the concern, passed in relative silence. It was because the chocolate maker went to great lengths to restore their slightly tarnished image and to return to a comfortable leadership position in its home country. Today, no one seems to dispute the fact that *Côte D'Or* is a Belgian company and that life as part of " the group " seems to be as sweet as ever. As proof, in 1999 the brand took up 40% of the market in Belgium while the factory in Halle produced more than 41,000 tonnes of chocolate, in all its forms.

Finally, for the record, know that 50% of the cocoa beans used by *Côte D'Or* are of what is called " noble " origin (that is, from Central and South America) while the others come from Africa.

Just between us...

As is the case for many Belgian companies, the Second World War considerably slowed the activities of *Côte d'Or*. The importation of cocoa was severely limited, while the quality of the cocoa that did make it in was clearly lower than before. So, *Côte D'Or* decided to suspend activities when the maker could no longer maintain the characteristic flavour of the brand's products. But the factory didn't stop and continued its activities under the name *Congobar*. The recipes were exactly the same as those used before the war but the origin of the cocoa was no longer guaranteed. *Congobar* survived until 1946.

A closer look at...

...the " *Temple du Chocolat* " (The Chocolate Temple). There are moments in life when we regret growing up so fast. One of those may come upon you once you know about this place reserved for elementary school pupils. The goal of this interactive museum is to teach children the route of the cocoa bean

Dessin d'enfant après une visite au Temple du Chocolat

A child's drawing after a visit at the Chocolate Temple

from harvest in a far away land to its transformation into chocolate. Numerous animations, grand stages and impressive visual effects capture the kiddies' attention. They can, in succession, visit a Toltec temple, explore the hold of a Spanish Galleon and follow the production steps in a reconstructed XIXth century chocolate shop. For a minute, they'll think they are at *Mickey's* house !

But that's not all : after the theory comes the practical exercise ! The students can test their skills as young chocolate makers, because it is possible for them to mould their own tablet of chocolate. Finally, the visit moves into the real factory where they can discover how the famous elephant gets stamped into the chocolate.

Parents can at least benefit from the descriptions their children return with, and if there's any left, taste the chocolate sweets that each pupil receives when leaving. And, if they insist on visiting these " off-limits " areas, then grown-ups will just have to become elementary school teachers...

DASKALIDES

Einde Were, 47
9000 Ghent
Tel. 09 225 35 37
Fax 09 224 01 78
e-mail : daskalides@skynet.be
http://www.daskalides.be
http://www.daskalides.com
Year founded: 1913

Export : 75% of production, mostly to France, the United States, Japan, the Middle East

Distribution : chain of stores, retailers,...

The Selection

What do Van Gogh, Rubens, Ensor, Monet, Picasso, Rembrandt and Cézanne have in common, other than the fact that they certainly all drag the brush better than the writer of this book ? Simple. They've all been remembered for posterity stamped into the form of a *Daskalidès* praline, among fifty other more conventional names. We can also pick out of the line-up one or two allusions to the owner's origins (*Athena*, *Flame*) and variations on that same theme (*Daska*-Mocha, *Daska*-Orange, *Daskananas* - pineapple).

Among the other products, let's note tablets, *napolitains*, bread spreads, jams, sea shells, and " Flow Packs " (to accompany coffee, personalized with your company's colours), available in boutiques with the sign from Ghent.

History

If Alexandre Daskalides prides himself on being a pure native of Ghent, he is also what we sometimes inappropriately call a third generation immigrant. His grandparents, the Daskalides – Kestekidis couple, arrived from their native Greece in Belgium, at the end of the 1920's. The choice of Belgium was not by chance, because the uncle of Madame Daskalides was none other than a certain...Leonidas Kestekidis, living with us in Belgium since 1913.

Thus was born, a fine day in 1931, the first Daskalides bakery-pastry shop in the town centre of Ghent. The success was so great that other boutiques, accompanied by tea-rooms, quickly appeared. The reputation of the chocolate making " side " of the business grew, so much so that in 1963, under the counsel of his son Jean, Prodromos abandoned pastry to devote himself solely to pralines.

In 1985, thanks to the wife of Jean, *Daskalides* broke out of the narrow confines of the Belgian borders to conquer the world. The popularity among the public was equal to his ambition, and still today, the number of outlets abroad continues to grow. As an example, they are almost to the record breaking number of 200 *Daskalides* points of sale in France, while the clearly stated goal is 500 over the coming years.

Quality without compromise

The pralines, though relatively few compared to the competition, are clearly targeted at the upper end of the market. Quality in fabrication is one of the governing principles of Alexandre Daskalides, today's leader who proudly states the different ingredients of certain pralines : fresh pineapple, kirsch, *" a good bottle of Armagnac or Batida "*, first quality nut meats, cream, soluble coffee, all the while rebelling against any artificial flavours.

As for comparisons, because they are inevitably made with its " cousin " *Leonidas*, we can simply say that the differences are essentially marked by a stronger attachment to family traditions, a greater perceived quality and a system of distribution that is not systematically executed through exclusive resellers.

Finally, since 1995, the chocolate maker from Ghent has become a company with two divisions : *Daskalides* and also *Alexandre*. This second brand benefits from the same high quality standards while offering pralines at a lower price.

Just between us...

We easily associate the name *Daskalides* with chocolate, pralines and to a certain extent already with other derivative products like spreads for morning toast. But would you have ever dreamed of a liqueur ? That may just be the case since one can now find a smooth whiskey cream, whose colour inevitably makes one think of a delicious chocolate...to be drunk in moderation just the same since it weighs in at 17% !

A closer look at...

...the ***Alexandre*** brand. After an examination of the tendencies in the marketplace, Alexandre Daskalidès saw that when sales stagnated, it wasn't so much a case of lassitude amongst the customers, but rather the fault of a lowering of their purchasing power. To remedy the situation, they had to target the lower end of the market, something that couldn't be permitted for the *Daskalides* brand. So, *Alexandre* was born, whose pralines are offered at a price about 40% lower in comparison to those charged by its big brother.

This difference in price was relatively simple to put into place : fewer fussy affectations, in the presentation of the packaging as well as the stores, and pralines whose final decoration are accomplished by hand. To make things a little easier, supplying the points of sale was confided to an independent distributor while the re-sellers systematically occupy a space in a heavily commercial zone. Up to the present, there are sixteen boutiques spread throughout Belgium.

DOLFIN

Chaussée de Tubize, 59
1440 Wauthier-Braine
Tel. 02 366 24 24
Fax 02 366 22 42
e-mail : dolfin@link.be
http://www.dolfin.be

Year founded: 1989

Export : 70% of production (European Union, Switzerland !, Canada, Asia,...)

Distribution : retailers (delicatessens, bakeries, pastry shops, restaurateurs,...)

The Selection

It was at *Dolfin* that we found originality expressed through chocolate. The selection is split into two camps : the *napolitains* and the tablets, each containing some astonishing flavours. So much so in fact, that a short listing is indispensable : Dark-Earl Grey, Dark-Mint, Milk-Javanese Cinnamon, Dark-Orange Rind and Lemon Rind, Dark-Amaretto, Dark-*Poire William*, Dark-Mandarin Napoléon, Dark-Fresh Ginger and finally, Dark-Pepper Rose...which the Petit Futé truly adored. Parallel to this, *Dolfin* offers several " strengths " of pure dark chocolates, running from 52% to 88%.

History

If one had to compare *Dolfin* to one of the La Fontaine fables, it certainly wouldn't be the one about the frog who thought he was a bull ! Though, its position among the true luxury products would justify it. But its founders, Michaël and Jean-François Poncelet put a lot more stock in the quality rather than the quantity produced. We should emphasise here that they are both from the " right school " since their father is none other than the one time director of the *Mondose*, *Corné Port-Royal*, and *Neuhaus* chocolate makers. From a quality point of view, it is hard to imagine a better apprenticeship.

On the other hand, they wanted to give a different spin to the " high-end " chocolate. In fact, *Dolfin* does not make fillings or other creams. That doesn't mean that there isn't a lot of variety to be had, quite the contrary ! We find 16 different types of " *napolitains* " (35 mm squares of 5 grams) and the same number of small tablets at 70g. The different " condiments " are added directly to the chocolate – without any processing beforehand – and add a more refined flavour and a more noticeable balance with the cocoa. This technique, more authentic according to its creators, allows combinations that are at the very least surprising, like that of chocolate and fresh ginger, the favourite of its " parents ".

Personalised machines

To ensure that they reach their goal, they didn't hesitate to modify, or even create new machines. To whit, the " *couleuse* " (pour-er) was built entirely from spare pieces, all the while placing quality at the head of their efforts.

Personalized "Napolitains".

Dolfin's products have less sugar and contain less fat and more cocoa than the average. Longevity gets a boost from this as well since it can be kept for over twelve months, although the production process uses absolutely no additives (preservative or colour). Finally, thanks to an elegant and very practical plastic package – debuted at an international salon in Paris – preservation after opening is assured.

On that subject, some malicious gossips say that it resembles a plain tobacco pouch, but don't believe them...there is no mention of *"Hazardous effects to one's health"* to be found on it !

Just between us...

Another of *Dolfin's* strong points rests in the personalisation of their product. From the beginning, the two brothers have integrated a print shop into their chocolate manufacture. This operation allows them not only to offer *napolitains* in the colours of companies, shops or associations who want to distinguish themselves, but also to make special packaging for occasions like Christmas, Easter or St. Valentine's Day. Among the clients of which *Dolfin* is most proud we find : *Hilton* hotels, the very hip Parisian restaurant *La Coupole* and even none other than...*British Airways* !

A closer look at...

...the liqueur " *napolitains* ". The creators of *Dolfin* certainly do not lack creativity. In fact, the famous squares just celebrated the arrival of three new members, named *Poire Williams, Mandarine Napoléon* and *Amaretto*. Specially designed to accompany the after meal coffee, these three sweets are made from dark chocolate, a crust of biscuit and a few drops of liqueur. Like the other products in the line, it is not a filling, which is rather rare for an alcoholic chocolate.

DRUART

Rue de Boughors, 13
7387 Angreau
Tel. 065 75 95 21
Fax 065 75 91 09

e-mail :
chocolat.druart@euronet.be
Year founded: 1982

Export : 70% of production (France, Great Britain, Denmark)

Distribution : 8 points of sale in Belgium (including the factory store)

The Selection

The artisan shop *Druart* offers an assortment of more than forty pralines, stuffed with fillings created in the shop. Beside the classics teems a series of originals : chocolate mousse, bitter almond mousse, *Cointreau* mousse, brown sugar cream, bitter squares with coriander, coconut perfumed with sugar cane alcohol, pistachio mousse, Irish Coffee, chocolate mousse with rum soaked raisins, butter-cream perfumed with Javanese chocolate, *ganaches* with tea, fresh lemon, fresh ginger, bitter squares with red wine, ... there are many others, some even better!

Finally, know too that Camille Druart offers many other resources : chocolate-hazelnut paste, dried fruit and nuts, *mignonnettes* 70%, *orangettes*, house-made *truffés* (including one with *Cointreau*), orchard fruit pastes, tablets made from single-crop chocolate and a praline of the month.

History

Back in 1982, the young graduate of the *Ecole Hôtelière de Namur*, Camille Druart was preparing to take the first steps of his professional career toward the great *Bocuse*, an unexpected event as sudden as it was passionate, kept him at home…

A few years earlier Camille's mother had chosen to fill the spare time of her young retired life by making chocolate. An apprenticeship with an older chocolate maker helped her decide to invest in the family's barn and, equipped with the minimum requisite materials, she began the production of her own pralines.

Chocolate for every sauce

An immediate success, redoubled by its shear extent, returned to compensate her hard work to such a degree that Madame Druart had to put her son's back to the wall (from where he could see the chocolate maker at work, of course…). Either he would take up his mother's business dealings, or she would have to drastically decrease production. Camille, a traveller always on the move, begged a short delay to ponder things and left to mull his decision in China. He met a young woman there, a doctor in mathematics. The charge passed so well between the two of them, that he brought her home along with his baggage and decided to…make her chocolates for the rest of her life.

Camille settled principally into the production of high-end pralines, something that doesn't keep him from having an opinion on chocolate in a larger sense.

He feels that one must strive for the flavour to be not too aggressive, but still adapt to the desires of the clientele. The geographical border situation of his chocolate factory supports him in this idea since the Belgians and the French have somewhat different concepts of chocolate. Camille Druart also likes to associate chocolate with certain other unusual ingredients such as thyme, laurel, basil or even... *kriek* ! And when the chocolate maker puts on his chef's hat, it is to simmer venison in a pepper sauce bound with butter and chocolate. Finally, Druart favours the association of chocolate and wine, and under this heading, suggests calmly tasting *truffés* accompanied by a nice red wine, or to allow yourself to be tempted by his latest creation : the bitter square with Bordeaux wine.

Despite the hubbub over the 5% vegetable fat, the maker from the Belgian Province of Hainaut continues to ply his trade with passion and to pursue his *œuvre* like a true professional. Being creative, he has made owls, squirrels, whales and golf tees. You can ask him if you would like something particular : Camille Druart takes pleasure in rendering them, as long as he finds the project amusing and morally correct ! In short, we find in this corner of Hainaut, the address of an undeniable great in Belgian chocolate making...

Just between us...

If one day you decide to pay a visit to the Druart Chocolate factory, don't be surprised if you see a nice limousine parked nearby. Seriously, you should know that Camille has gained certain enthusiasts among the elite. So, you find among his current and past clientele certain personages that are more than famous : heads of State and government figures, actors,...whose notoriety long ago spread beyond the borders of Europe.

A closer look at...

...*Mathilde* ! This ganache perfumed with rose was created by *Druart* on the occasion of the *Triumphant Entry* of the new princely couple to Mons.

DUC D'O

Bazelstraat, 250
9150 Kruibeke
Tel. 03 774 51 91
Fax 03 774 40 56
e-mail : info@ducdo.com
http://www.ducdo.com
Year founded: 1983
Export : 85% of production
Distribution : large and medium sized markets, pastry shops, grocers, ...

The Selection

The production of *Duc d'O* is spread among three fairly classic categories. The " Baker's Pralines " are composed of basic fillings like : *praliné*, hazelnut truffle, orange cream or pistachio cream, or even marzipan and caramel. The packaged pralines include under their banner the milk and white chocolate *truffés*, *praliné* hearts, liqueur chocolates, and others baptised " *La Boule Duc d'O* ". Finally, the chocolate maker from Flanders offers the *Fruits d'O*, fruit jellies (strawberry, raspberry, grape, pear, orange) coated with dark chocolate.

History

The adventure began when Hendrik Verhelst created his own chocolate making enterprise by buying three chocolate production lines from the chocolate maker *Guylian*. The beginning was hard work, though promising. Then, in a usable space of 16,145 ft², the chocolate maker produced in total 3.5 tonnes daily, covering three categories : pralines, *truffés* and liqueurs. Starting in 1986, construction works and modifications began on a roughly annual basis over about ten years, which allowed the production capacity to multiply. The enterprise now inhabits an area of 323,000 ft², twenty times that of its beginnings, and is capable of producing 30 tonnes of diverse varieties of chocolate per day. This development also allows the employment of 60 permanent positions and up to 170 during the busiest times.

The success of *Duc d'O* chocolate is perhaps due to the quality and preservation possibilities of its products. The coating chocolate (*chocolat de couverture)* is none other than *Callebaut* (why not mention it, since it is such a quality product...). Elsewhere, tests conducted in the heart of the enterprise demonstrated that the liqueur filled chocolates could be kept for a minimum of six months while the other varieties can be kept for a year without problem. Is the secret of this freshness guarantee the addition of several preservatives ? Absolutely not, of course. *Duc d'O* simply uses a particular method of packaging, which accomplishes the sealing of the chocolates in less than one minute.

Outside of Europe, *Duc d'O* is present in North America, Argentina, South Africa, the Middle East and in Australia.

A closer look at...

... the " liqueurs ". *Duc d'O* offers a complete array of dark chocolates filled with liqueurs. The aesthetic aspect of the presentation is assured thanks to the placing of the chocolates in a fitted wooden container reminiscent of those used for bottles, as well as coloured wrappings. But the most important aspect is on the inside. Because we're not talking about just any old " liqueurs ", but the great names like *Grand Marnier, Cointreau, Mandarine Napoléon, Cognac Otard* or *Courvoisier* and *Whisky VAT 69.* To add an extra note of charm to these sweets, *Duc d'O* reproduced on each praline a miniature version of the label from the bottles of liqueur noted. An original gift idea...except for a member of A.A.!

GALLER

rue de la Station, 39
4051 Vaux-sous-Chèvremont
Tel. 04 367 22 11
Fax 04 365 92 20
e-mail : infos@galler.com
http://www.galler.com

Year founded: 1976

Export : 15% of production (notably to Switzerland)

Distribution : large and average sized markets, specialty boutiques, 4 stores in Brussels, Liège, Wavre and Vaux-sous-Chèvremont

The Selection

No need to cover the "classic" products from Galler, since they are largely described in these few lines. Rather, did you know that the maker offers four delicious spreads (*Praliné, Café, Génoise* and *Chocolat*) as well

Langues de chat...

as "*bouchées*" ("mouthfuls") and "*caraques" (chocolate disks covered with fruit and nuts) ? Otherwise, you will surely be familiar with the famous Langues de Chat* (literally "Cat's Tongues"), festively packaged with the complicity of Philippe Geluck (the creator of the comic strip *Le Chat* – The Cat). Closed up in their metallic boxes, they are 18 in number and are available in *praliné*-milk chocolate, white chocolate and fondant chocolate, as well as " extreme " dark chocolate. In short, the Cat is Content...

History

The history of the chocolate maker Galler started out a little like a fairy tale. At the age of sixteen, Jean Galler left the *Ecole Hôtelière de Liège* to follow an apprenticeship at a bakery, then pastry shop, and in so doing taking up a familial heritage begun by his grandfather and followed by his own father. He discovered a true passion for chocolate and installed a little manufacturing set up in the cellar of his parent's house. Maybe this is what drew him to apply at Bâle, so that he could complete his education and crack the secrets of the master Swiss chocolate makers. Finally, he finished his schooling in Paris, at the side of Gaston Lenôtre himself.

We are now in 1976 and, again in the region of Liège, Jean Galler took advantage of the extraordinary opportunity to buy the facilities of the *Clovis* chocolate maker in Vaux-sous-Chèvremont. The purchase price was obviously high, but the benefits would no doubt be worth the candle. In association with his father, who rapidly put an end to his baking activities, he thusly created the *Chocolaterie Galler*.

Bars, lots of bars...

Jean Galler could let his imagination run wild and different forms of chocolate were born rapidly. Among these, the 70g (2.5oz) bar appears, and is still today the most in demand and probably most appreciated of the *Galler* line. It is now available in 23 different varieties. Most are completely original creations. We site notably the *Piémontais*, which is a milk chocolate filled with hazelnuts from Piedmont, puffed rice and coconut ; the *Mandarine*, made with a clear mousse of *Mandarine Napoléon* and sprinkled with candied orange bits,

Chocolate soup by Galler

not to forget the *Café Liégeois* (the Petit Futé's favourite), built on a base of mousse, lightly perfumed with coffee and covered in fondant chocolate. All these bars are offered in the same manner (four pieces, in a wrapper that is sober but at the same time colourful) and make use of dark, white and/or milk chocolate.

As for the tablets, originality resides there as well. The format (100g or 3.5oz) is somewhat old fashioned in Belgium, the flavours mostly follow the beaten track and recall natural products, like vanilla bean.

...but there are also the pralines

As for pralines, they are distinguishable by their size (they are small in order to satisfy the gourmet) as well as by their original names and fillings. They contain only natural ingredients like vanilla bean, noble cocoa beans, Earl Grey tea and fresh pistachios.

The Manon, which every good " *pralineur* " or praline maker must offer, sets itself apart from its brothers in name with its low concentration of sugar and small pieces of nuts. What else can we say about the *Mazarine* (*truffé* with *Mandarine Napoléon*), *Amadou* (*truffé* with almond paste), *Oasienne* (orange-almond paste), *Maury* (*truffé* with *Mas d'Amiel*) or the *Mazagran* (coffee-caramel), except that they delight our taste buds by just pronouncing their names.

And as for the packaging, the " *ballotin* " was specially designed to be opened easily, manipulated frequently and protect the little beauties inside for a long time. Along the same idea, the different layers in the box are easily accessible, permitting the curious to "voyage" into the interior. These same people will be happy to learn that they can create their own variety boxes and the eternally undecided can benefit from boxes packed in advance and kept ready in a refrigerated room.

Just between us...

Fans of police fiction will certainly know the famous "Pendu de Saint-Pholien" ("The Hanged Man from Saint-Pholien"), of which the hero is the no less famous *Commissaire Maigret*. What is perhaps less well known is that it refers to a district of Liège, in the *République Libre d'Outre-Meuse* (Free Republic of Outre-Meuse). What's this got to do with chocolate you ask ? Simply the appellation of one of these numerous pralines, justly named *Saint-Pholien*. Jean Galler thereby underlines, with a wink of his eye, his *liégitude* (don't bother looking it up in the dictionary, it's a word with a very unique usage...).

A closer look at...

...the *Chocolate-Tea* rooms. One can imagine, even without knowing him, the love that Jean Galler brings to chocolate. It is, however, less easy to guess another almost identical passion of his for tea. Add to this a certain penchant for humour and you will quickly find the origin of these signposts with the *double-entendre*. *Chocolate-Tea* (also a homophone in French, that means *chocolaty*) is cocoa in all of its states, available in every possible form. They are, in fact, restaurants where you can select your meal from among dishes containing cocoa, from the aperitif through the...dessert (of course !). Among the different specialties offered *spices and bitter chocolate.* we find the *cocoa soup* (see *Chocolate & Cuisine*), *terrine of fish in cabbage leaves, mustard sauce and white chocolate sauce, sliced foie-gras in terrine, Maury wine and extreme dark chocolate sauce* and even *chicken with sweet*

Jean Galler hoped, by his own admission, to make these places reminiscent of his childhood and above all the cooking of his grand mother. But outside of this purely culinary aspect, it is possible to drop into a *Chocolate-Tea* at any time of day. There you can sample different types of hot chocolate, prepared in the traditional manner (notably from recipes out of the XIVth, XVIth and XVIIIth centuries) as well as more than 30 different kinds of tea, dear to the owner's heart.

On the inside, there is also the *Chocolate-Show* space (again a play on words for a *double-entendre Chocolate-Show* is a homophone in French for *chocolat chaud* which means "hot chocolate"), that allows the curious to discover the different steps in the transformation of cocoa, from the bean to the tablet. These veritable Ali Baba's caves number just two at the moment : one in Uccle and the other in Namur.

GODIVA

Rue de l'Armistice, 5
1081 Brussels
Tel. 02 422 17 11

Fax 02 422 17 00
e-mail : letters@godiva.com
http://www.godiva.com
Year founded: 1946
Export : 80% of total volume (2.160 tonnes in 99-2000)
Distribution : special distribution channels

The Selection

Despite a good half century of existence, Lady Godiva still has some beautiful jewels. Her selection is rich with fifty different types of pralines, of which half are composed of different *pralinés*. Some of these are available in both dark and milk chocolate versions, like the *Cœur de Bruxelles* (Heart of Brussels), the *Amandine* (Almond) or the *Huître* (Oyster).
A few other specialties carry names much in line with the standing of the house : *Comtesse*, *Elysée*, *Fabiola* or *Palet d'Or*, *Saint Germain*, *Hamlet* and *Raisin Fine Champagne*. Five *truffés* complete a family that also has traditional ganaches and caramels, crèmes fraîches and marzipans...don't forget the *Manon Blanc* and *Manon Café*.

History

In the 1920's, Pierre Draps installed his chocolate confectionary in Brussels and began the production of pralines, mostly destined for large stores. These then re-sold them under their own brands. When he reached the age of fourteen, Joseph Draps joined his father's business and quickly started to show his *savoir-faire* in that domain.
In 1946, once the war stopped, it was with his wife, Gabriella, at his side that he created the *Godiva* brand, whose fame now circles the globe. This was the original objective of its creators. So they chose a trade name for their enterprise that stood out, and was easily pronounced in most foreign languages. *Godiva* pleased them, not only for the sympathetic legend that it evoked but also because, according to them, the name carried a feeling of luxury and quality.
Quickly, Joseph Draps developed a network of stores all over the country. They all adopted the same style : luxurious decoration and themed window dressings that changed frequently. according to, for instance, bank holidays or the seasons. The principle hit the bull's-eye, so that in just a few years, *Godiva* made a special place for itself in the world of Belgian chocolate.

A star is born

Twelve years after its creation, in 1958, *Godiva* made its triumphant entry into Paris, and since 1966, 5th Avenue in New York has been home to the first American boutique. Today *Godiva* uses, in addition to its Brussels facilities, a second production line in Pennsylvania, serving no less than 1,200 points of sale. But *Godiva's* interest in the United States is no coincidence : in 1974 the firm was purchased by the *Campbell's* group, most famous for its soup cans that were painted by

Andy Warhol. Nonetheless, freedom of action for *Godiva* has been, and is still, intact.
On this topic, the criteria for production and, above all for finishing, laid out by Joseph Draps are almost all unchanged. The decoration of the pralines is still done in large part by hand and even the heavy machines haven't completely replaced manual labour.
Moreover, we mustn't forget the fact that Godiva has 54 boutiques in Belgium and is present in the large majority of European countries, notably France, Spain, Portugal and Italy. Across the globe, outside of the " pied-à-terre " in North America, we should point out the presence of the majestic Lady in Brazil, the Arab Emirates, Japan (Tokyo is the third commercial entity in the group) and in Russia where the Muscovites have just recently discovered the pleasures of Belgian chocolate. Finally, *Godiva* pralines are available in most duty-free shops on the planet.

Just between us...

Do you know Emile ? The master chocolate maker, and veritable champion in the art of *trempage* (dipping), ceaselessly runs among the world's *Godiva* boutiques. Each time, he starts with the same little game : completing, by hand, the decoration of pralines, in front of the future customer of the delicious specialties. It would be hard to find anything fresher...

A closer look at...

...the *Autant.* Its real name is none other than " *Autant en Emporte le Vent* " (" Gone with the Wind "), directly inspired by one of the most famous movies in the history of American cinema. This praline was created in the 40's (even before the official appearance of the *Godiva* appellation) on the occasion of the film's opening in Brussels. Its delicious filling (coffee cream and cognac) is covered in milk chocolate and topped with...a stylised version of the feather decorating Scarlett's hat.

GUYLIAN

Europark-Oost, 1
9100 Sint-Niklaas
Tel. 03 760 97 00
Fax 03 777 06 81
e-mail : guymail@guylian.be
http://www.guylian.be
Year founded: 1960
Export : 95% of production, to 5 continents (140 countries)
Distribution : large stores, special retailers, duty free shops, service stations,...

Chocolate concerto.

Too good

to give away.™

GuyLian®

CREATIONS IN CHOCOLATE

www.guylian.be

The Selection

The Guylian selection is composed of 5 families of chocolates. The most famous among them, the *Fruits de Mer* (Seashells) series, translates as marbled pralines (white, dark and milk chocolate), sculpted in the form of seashells and filled with hazelnut *praliné*.
The others are called *La Perlina* (8 pralines sculpted by a jeweller, filled with a cappuccino cream, and each one surrounding a whole hazelnut), *La Trufflina* (*truffé* pralines, covered with grains of white, dark or milk chocolate), *Opus* (an assortment of 8 pralines on the theme of great opera classics) and *Solitaire*. This fawn coloured box holds several varieties of dark chocolate *napolitains*, each made from cocoa beans of a different origin, but not blended.

History
Who isn't familiar with the famous chocolate *Fruits de Mer* (Seashells) ? We mean, of course, the chocolates dreamt up by Guy and Liliane Foubert shortly after their marriage in 1960, according to a recipe developed two years earlier. This is also how the chocolate maker *Guylian* was born, whose name, of course, is a contraction of the two names.

The enterprise began with the production of pralines and *truffés*, that the couple would take out and sell on their own in the market places. But something quickly made itself clear : the *truffés* were poor sellers outside of the winter months. After a short period of reflection, Guy Foubert struck upon the idea of making pralines in the shape of seashells, and thereby ensuring his initial success...on the Belgian coast ! Sales soared to a point that in 1988 a brand new production site was inaugurated.

Today, *Guylian's Fruits de Mer*, as well as their other products, are exported to 140 other countries (68% of which goes to the heart of the European Union). In the same spirit, 58% of *duty free* shops sell *Guylian* chocolates, a sector in which the brand is easily the Belgian leader. Add to that the commercial presence in 10 countries : France, Germany, Austria, Spain, Italy, Great Britain, Portugal, the United States, Canada and Japan. Finally, *Guylian* claims to be on top of the Belgian market for pre-packaged pralines. All this to show why 1998 was truly the year of devotion and recognition, as *Guylian* received an *Export Award,* bestowed by the Belgian Office of Foreign Commerce (*OBCE*). This magnifi-

Soyez bien sages, nous allons lever le rideau !

Be good, we're going to raise the curtain!

cent distinction repays the recognition that *Guylian* has brought to Belgium and honours its position as number one among exporters.
Modern daily production has risen to…75 tonnes in factories that now cover 269,000 ft^2 and are completely up to date, with an application for ISO 9002 certification. The production is achieved entirely in the factory in Sint-Niklaas. This is how *Guylian* could remain true to its initial objectives : offer a quality product at a reasonable price and accessible to all the rungs of the population, who have now discovered that other things exist besides the *Fruits de Mer*.

Fruits de Mer to the hippocampus' rescue

The last few years, *Guylian* has developed a whole array to sit alongside its fetish chocolates. *La Truffina* was born in 1992 and the *Opus* line began in 1995, followed one year later by the *La Perlina* assortment. One can also find *Guylian* chocolates in the form of pleasantly filled eggs around Easter.
If you didn't pay much attention, you might think that all the *Fruits de Mer* look alike. However, *Guylian* offers 11 different forms arranged around the same theme. The best known of the assortment is probably the hippocampus, which partially explains *Guylian's* involvement in *Project Seahorse*. The Canadian project concerns the safeguarding of the hippocampus, these little " Seahorses ", which figure into the economies of 47 countries around the globe. The market for these animals, alive or dead, along with intensive fishing, would have lowered by half the overall numbers of the species over the last five years. *Guylian* became associated with the Sea Horse Project, led by Dr Amanda Vincent and Dr Heather Hall. The chocolate maker has agreed to free up 750,000 dollars over five years

Old chocolate-vending machine

to help lead this effort, which seeks above all to control strictly, rather than disallow, trade. Finally, *Guylian* also offers a powerful communication outlet to the association, by giving them an opportunity to express their cause on the chocolate's packages and boxes.

But don't let any of this keep you from continuing to eat the chocolate hippocampus, from *Guylian*: there are no restrictions foreseen on that...

Just between us...

How can you recognize a real *Guylian Fruit de Mer* ? The solution is easy, the original pralines must be embellished with a "G", moulded into the chocolate. *Voilà*, an easily performed method of *copyrighting* that one only need think about...

A closer look at...

... the *Opus* line. This original *Guylian* creation was born in 1995 and easily set itself apart from the other products of the brand. It was completely re-thought a few months ago. There are eight *Opus* pralines and hereafter owe their names to eight famous operas. They are as follows :

Roméo et Juliette : a *praliné* with hazelnut in the shape of a heart (of course) and packaged in gold wrapping.

La Flûte Enchantée (*The Magic Flute*) : a flute made of white and milk chocolate in which a whole hazelnut is imprisoned.

Madame Butterfly : a marbled chocolate butterfly, surrounding an orange cream.

La Fille du Régiment (The Daughter of the Regiment): another whole hazelnut covered in milk chocolate shaped like a drum...with sticks.

Aïda : a *truffé* praline in a triangular shape, on which the sphinx is enthroned in relief.

Toccata et Fugue : a small ingot of gianduja covered in dark chocolate, striped with white.

Sonate au Clair de Lune : a disc of milk chocolate filled with cappuccino, topped with a half-moon of white chocolate and decorated with stars and musical notes.

Manon : easily more classic than its sisters from the same box, as much in shape as in name. But this white chocolate striped with fine dark chocolate lines reminds us that *Manon* was first and foremost an opera (Massenet – 1884) and a comic-opera (Puccini – 1893).

ITALO-SUISSE

Avenue des Châteaux, 107a
7780 Comines
Tel. 056 56 05 05
Fax 056 55 66 76
e-mail : contact@italosuisse.com
http://www.italosuisse.com
Year founded: 1923
Export : Benelux, France, England, the United States, Germany
Distribution : large stores, small retailers, bakeries, service stations,...

History

The father of Joseph Dequeker was a pastry chef in Izegem (Western Flanders). When his son was old enough, and showed a desire to integrate into the family business, he felt that he needed a more professional apprenticeship and sent him abroad to school. And so, Joseph ended up in Marseille, where he officiated as a cook.

The success was greater than before, so good in fact that the brand was re-baptised in order to help expansion throughout Flanders : *Italo-Suisse* was born. In 1963, new expansion works were necessary and in 1975 it was in Comines, on the outskirts of Hainaut, that the enterprise finally landed. This last move coincided with the passing of power to the third generation, still at the helm today. The years 1989, 1992, 1995 and 1997 were also periods full of evolutions, expansions and new creations. Finally, the future King Albert II honoured *Italo-Suisse* with his princely visit in 1991.

Quality, nothing but quality

The four children of Antoine Libeert each head up a specified section : Ignace is commercial director, Luc supervises production, Pieter is in charge of finances while Myriam handles the artistic part (design,...). Today more than ever, as the European Union has made important decisions about the use of cocoa butter, *Italo-Suisse* wants to be a chocolate maker that respects tradition. The methods of production have always conformed to our image of quality chocolate. There are several international prizes that attest to this, including a *Master d'Or* and another silver at the 1999 European competition, and ISO 9001 certification which is being finalised as the present guide is being buttoned up.

Next, he left for Italy, where he was taught the art of making candied chestnuts. His path led him next to Switzerland, the country where he discovered the techniques of the chocolate maker's trade.

Returning to Belgium in 1923, Dequeker simply installed himself a few dozen metres from the family pastry shop and called his chocolate shop " Spécialités Suisses et Italiennes " (Swiss and Italian Specialties) thereby paying homage to his teachers. In 1938, the enterprise moved the first time to Roulers. In 1950, after reconstruction due to war damage, the second generation, consisting of Antoine Libeert and his wife, started up operations.

But let's talk about chocolate ! *Italo-Suisse* is known above all for its seasonal moulds, of which the enterprise is one of the largest Belgian producers. Dressed in dark, white or milk chocolate, they decorate the store aisles at critical times like *Saint-Nicolas*, Christmas and Easter. There are so many diverse effigies that children (the primary consumers of this type of chocolate) have too many from which to choose.

Aside from this fairly " temporal " selection, *Italo-Suisse* also produces its own brand of tablets (five kinds) and markets pralines under the names *Isis* and *Azur*.

Just between us...

Do you dream of a chocolate moulded in your likeness, or more seriously, would you like to market bars or tablets under a specific name ? *Italo-Suisse* can take on the production for you, after evaluating the ideal production quantities. It is even possible to create an original recipe, just as it is possible to get packaging specific to your wishes. In the same spirit, *Italo-Suisse* has adapted to the different export markets. That is why the little bunnies that arrive in Japan at Christmas time have culturally appropriate designs...

JACALI

Brugsesteenweg, 95
8450 Bredene
Tel. 059 34 03 30
Fax 059 34 03 31
Year founded: 1988
Export : 75% of sales in +/- 50 countries
Distribution : small retailers, large distribution

Old steel moulds

The Selection

Fairly classic but devilishly well endowed, the productions of *Jacali* include the irresistible pralines with crème fraîche, ganache, marzipan, *praliné* and lastly gianduja from among which we pull these original appellations : *Noëlla*, *Ginger*, *Marquise*, *Rembrandt*, *Cléopâtre*, *Carré Blanc* (White Square) and *Stanjol* just to name these few. At their side, *Jacoli* offers a small collection of bars, among which five are filled (*Cappuccino*, *Brésilienne* (Brazilian), *Praliné Lait* (Milk Chocolate *Praliné*), *Praliné Noir* (Dark Chocolate *Praliné*), *Praliné Blanc* (White Chocolate *Praliné*)). Finally, the chocolate maker from the seaside produces numerous other specialties like *Mendiants* (dried fruits and nuts), *Caraques* (a disk of chocolate covered with dried fruit and nuts), *Orangettes*, *Truffés*, *Langues de Chat* ("Cat's Tongues "),...

History

When, on 8th August 1988, Jaak and Carl Lingier set up the foundations of the *Jacali* chocolate business, they were resurrecting a certain family tradition. Indeed, as early as 1922 their grand father and great uncle, Jaak and Karel Lingier, began the production of chocolate in a truly artisan manner (in the cellars of their houses), and continued up until the Second World War broke out. In 1962, Edgar Lingier, son and nephew of the preceding, took up the family business for a while and developed the enterprise. These activities took on an even larger aspect with the creation of *Jacali* in 1988.

Though the founders first hope was to ensure solid marketing of their chocolate via their own bulk trade, other bulk confectionary agents quickly showed interest in *Jacali*. With their success to help them, the Lingier brothers decided to test the waters outside of Belgium, which up until then had been the boundary of their sales territory.

But their chocolates in bulk didn't take flight as expected when exported, something that led Carl and Jaak to develop an assortment of pre-packaged chocolates. It was such a success that today it is the largest line of production at *Jacali*.

This mostly wild progression of sales obliged Jacali to move to a larger space, which was accomplished in 1997 with the construction of a more than 100,000 ft^2 factory. The little enterprise has since had 45 employees as full time workers, who are joined by another 50 during periods of intense production.

Finally, outside of its own chocolate production, Jacali also makes chocolate for other brands.

Just between us...

Some may think this isn't top drawer information, but we are pleased to point out the politeness and professionalism of the personnel at *Jacali*. This chocolate maker may be far from the most renowned or important of all those in our kingdom, but some of its competitors, sometimes more popular, could learn

Chocolate factory Jacques in Verviers (Belgium).

a thing or two! Be assured that they know the value of pleasant human interaction up in Bredene...

A closer look at...

...personalised products. Like all the other chocolate makers in the world, Jacali makes figurines or special shapes for certain occasions. We pass the more traditional, bunnies, bells and chicks, though they are different in that they are solid chocolate from smallish moulds. To remember, we site the snowmen (the three usual variations, plus one marbled) as well as special Christmas *caraques* with multiple facets.

However, they become rather original when we get to the eggs for Easter. There are still the familiar coverings (White, Milk and Dark), but we must add two more original creations. The first is made of dark or milk chocolate on one half, with coloured fondant sugar on the other half egg. In the same spirit, the second marriage is composed of the same types of chocolate and jelly, like that used to make mice or little bears.

Finally, we can't keep the chocolate asparagus secret, made of dark and white chocolate, truer than nature...

JACQUES

Industriestrasse,16
4700 Eupen
Tel. 087 59 29 11
Fax 087 59 29 50
e-mail : info@chocojacques.be
Year founded: 1896
Export : 80% of production
Distribution : large markets, bulk dealers, small businesses (bakeries, grocers, book stores,...)

The Selection

Jacques offers the traditional array of a Belgian chocolate maker : milk chocolate and hazelnut tablets, white or fondant chocolate, almonds or *praliné*...everything is there ! They've added to that two tablets from " Grand Crus " with noble origins, one dark and the other a milk chocolate version. The chocolate making habits of this brand are best shown by their chocolate bars. Dressed in new outfits, they are almost all filled with different creams : banana, three fruit, orange, peach, tropical, and also mocha rum and double rum, *praliné* and marzipan. Finally, *Kiko*, *Twinko* and *Krako* are small bars with milk cream, principally directed at the younger public.

History

In 1896, Antoine Jacques founded, in Verviers, a chocolate making business that carried his name. This wasn't his first outing since, associated with a certain Hardy, he had already started activities in 1890, making chocolates, gingerbreads and confections under the brand name " *Le Semeur* " (The Sower). From the beginning they were able to capitalize on available specialised labour, since the town supported several similar businesses.

In 1920, after the tragic death of his son, Antoine Jacques struck up an association with William Zurstrassen and together, they founded the *S.A. Chocolaterie Jacques.* Two years later, the factory up and re-installed itself in Eupen, in

the German speaking region of Belgium.
On 8th February, 1936, *Jacques* was to, without realizing it, revolutionize the world of chocolate by registering a patent : he was, in fact, the first to think of creating bars of chocolate with fillings, which were to please many generation of pupils. Today, the bars are a sure bet...and THE specialty of the business.

The big adventure of little pictures

Right after the invention of the filled chocolate bar, *Jacques* returned to his first love. The chocolate maker had in effect initiated the movement back at the beginning of the XXth century : while it was still made under the name " Le Semeur ", the chocolate from Eupen offered its clients little pictures called *chromos*. These vignettes had themes as diverse as birds, plants, cocoa cultivation and many other things.

Also, while the filled bars were taking flight, they were systematically accompanied by a little sticker that could be kept in special albums. This continued for about forty years, right up to the beginning of the eighties. Many generations of children were led by this to their favourite sport : bartering. There is no doubt that not a single playground in the country escaped the tradition.
This type of exchange followed elsewhere and in other domains, notably with the *Pannini* images (certainly more lucrative for their creators, since you had to buy these and they came along with...nothing else in exchange !) while the *children of the year 2000* all squabble over *Pokémons* and *Simpsons*. But let's not wander, back to *Jacques*. For several years, the *Kiko*, *Krako* and *Twinko* bars, particularly targeted at the youngest, have returned the *chromos* to favour

Chocolate factory Jacques in Verviers (Belgium).

somewhat by offering a mini-collection of images with the *Petit Spirou* character.

A rather lively centenarian

Since 1982, the *Chocolaterie Jacques* has depended on the Stollwerck group, a multinational with its headquarters in Cologne. This re-grouping was beneficial for the company from Eupen since sales haven't stopped climbing since that time. The growth in production has led to the construction of a new production site, which has been in operation since July 1987. That same factory was enlarged by 50% in 1994.
In 1993, the Walloon Region bestowed an award on the chocolate maker to repay their efforts in export. The same year, they reached the European quality norm ISO 9002. The century mark (1996) was the occasion for installing a new quality control system.
Another peculiarity of the company is its laboratory installed in the heart of the enterprise. The Research and Development department allows the creation of new products, and provides quality and sanitation analysis on both finished and semi-finished products. Elsewhere, *Jacques* accomplishes all of the stages of chocolate production except the roasting, which is confided to the Berlin branch of the group. Environmentally sensitive, the *Chocolaterie Jacques* watches over the health of its customers and its surroundings...since it has no immediate neighbours, which removes the possibility of creating a noise nuisance.

Inaugurated in 1994, the ***Musée du Chocolat*** (Museum of Chocolate) permits those interested to combine a visit to modern installations with some of the history of cocoa. The

Chocolate pot in Sèvres china 1940.

" *Maison du Chocolat* " (House of Chocolate) gives everyone a chance to take away some delicious souvenirs (filled bars, tablets, marzipans, biscuits,...).

Just between us...

Did you know that *Jacques* is also a producer of coating chocolate *(chocolat de couverture)* for biscuit, praline and ice cream makers ? They supply in all 40% of their production to other confectioners and biscuit makers. In this category, the enterprise makes up, along with *Callebaut* and *Belcolade*, the trio of principle Belgian chocolate producers.

A closer look at...

...what's new. On the occasion of its centenary, the firm from Eupen launched three new specialties : *Praliné 100*, *Biscuité 100* and *Nuts 100* came out into the light of day, presented in

packaging that harkens back to the original.
The 150g (5.3oz) tablets *Praliné Lait* (milk *praliné*) appeared in 1997, joining the delicious original *Praliné Noir* (dark chocolate). At the same time, the *Grand Cru Fondant* was born, weighing in at 72% cocoa, the 25g (0.88oz) bars *(Milk* and *Broken Hazelnut*), *Fondant Orange* and the *Mini-Jacques*, go so well with a small black coffee, taken on the terrace.
The passing of the year 2000 was the occasion to introduce the new filled bars *Fondant Pêche* (Peach) and *Tropical Milk*. The *Jacques* chocolate maker took advantage of the occasion to refresh its image by giving its new creations new, more up to date packaging.

KATHY

Pathoekweg, 84
8000 Bruges
Tel. 050 32 06 92
Fax 050 32 02 01
Year founded: 1919
Export : 70% of production
Distribution : large distribution

The Selection

The *Kathy* chocolate company specialises in making " industrial " pralines, in coloured individual wrappers, and available in bulk in a metallic box.

History
In 1919, August Verheecke created a confectioner's in the Venice of the North. All the evidence points to a smashing popularity ; three moves or expansions took place before 1945, in the early history of Kathy. In that year, the son, Georges Verheecke took over operation of the company upon the death of its founder. With the public demand helping, the pralines pulled ahead of the other products from the confectioner and in 1979 several divisions, including a chocolate making division, were created from the original enterprise.
The eighties were growth years, as much for the administration of the company (which re-structured and organised itself better) as for the export markets, on which the majority of *Kathy's* production centred. The principle importing countries were locally limited in the beginning (the Netherlands, France and Germany, to which we should add the United Kingdom) but since then Kathy chocolates are being exported to many countries all over the world.
Finally, outside of the products marketed under their own brand, Kathy also makes chocolate for some big clients. In 2001, the turnover should reach 1 thousand million Belgian francs.

KIM'S CHOCOLATES

Nieuwelandlaan, 12
3200 Aarschot
Tel. 016 55 15 80
Fax 016 56 92 42
e-mail : info@kimchoc.be
Year founded: 1987
Export : sold in more than 40 countries
Distribution : special agents, bulk retailers, large distribution

Product selection

In *Les Cygnes* (The Swans), *Kim's Chocolate* offers a selection both wide and varied, proposing the praline in a full range of different flavours. It is

impossible to list here each of the almost 90 creations of the brand, but we can't help but take at least a peek. In the praline category then, we single out the fillings like mandarin, cinnamon, bolts of cocoa and puffed rice, while the ganaches promise sublime moments thanks to several interiors with different liqueurs. On the crème fraîche and butter cream side, we must underline the surprising strawberry – marzipan, chestnut – rum, and date puree. Finally, one might enjoy the presence of several yoghurt pralines, as well as fondant mint or lemon, and macerated raisins, among the other original flavours.

History

The least we can say is that the little enterprise, founded in 1987, has really grown ! *Kim's Chocolate* today proudly posts a turnover of 520 million Belgian francs and deploys activities over an area of 75,350 ft². The enterprise has 3 lines of production reaching a capacity of 4,000 tonnes in 1999.

Among the subjects close to the Brabant chocolate maker's heart, the quality of the products and contact with the clientele come immediately to mind. They can be justifiably proud of being the first artisan chocolate maker in Europe to receive ISO 9002 certification, in June 1993.

Three varieties but a single spirit

The production of *Kim's Chocolate* is available in three distinct varieties: *Orfeuille*, *Cachet* and *Les Cygnes*. This last one, completely overhauled in September 2000, has its own distribution network and reflects, according to its founders, an image that is modern and classic at the same time. As proof, their logo represents two interlaced and stylised swans in a mix of grey and white. The assortment covers more than 80 pralines, prepared exclusively with a base of cocoa butter and whose fillings are made from scratch in the heart of the chocolate shop. Finally, they contain no OGM and are kosher.

Orfeuille is the name given to the line of chocolate bars directed at special retailers and comprised of 9 different tastes. As for the *Cachet* line, it was completely...melted down and re-shaped in January 2001. Since then, it is composed of an assortment of packaged pralines with hand made fillings. Among these interiors, the ganaches, marzipans and *pralinés* rival the creams, fondants and caramels. Finally, the *Cachet* pralines benefit from a luxurious and new exclusive assortment : nut creams, chocolate waffles and 70% dark chocolate.

Just between us...

To help you make your way through the intricacies of the *Les Cygnes* product line, *Kim's* has definitely thought of everything. Each praline is easily identifiable thanks to its name : the first initial of each shows the category to which it belongs. *Primavera* or *Paso Doble* are then *pralinés*, *Ghiotto* and *Gulliver* belong to the ganaches while *Mathilde*...is an appetising white chocolate filled with pistachio marzipan.

LEONIDAS

Boulevard Jules Graindor, 43
1070 Brussels
Tel. 02 522 19 57
Fax 02 522 09 43
e-mail : info@leonidas.com
http://www.leonidas.be
Year founded: 1913
Export : 1750 points of sale all over the world
Distribution : Leonidas has its own distribution network, via franchised and independent boutiques

The Selection

The most popular praline maker in Belgium offers a wide but classic selection of more than 80 pralines, whose originality lies mostly in the selection of names : *Mystère* or *Desires*, *Eve* or *Antoinette*, *Tosca* or *Poésie* (Poetry), *Louise* or *Casanova*. On that same track, we'd like to point out that *Princesse Enrobée* (Coated Princess) and *Princesse Moulée* (Moulded Princess) are also two specialties under the Leonidas hallmark...no insult intended ! Most of the pralines are available with either milk or dark chocolate coating. The selection is rounded out by a large array of seasonal products.

History

Léonidas...a funny name for a Belgian chocolate maker, don't you think ? Don't look too hard for a mystery, its founder, Leonidas Kestekidis, was Greek. At the beginning of the century that we just recently closed, he immigrated to the country of Uncle Sam, where he began his chocolate making activities.

The first time Kestekidis set foot on Belgian soil was in 1910 : he was participating in the Brussels World Fair, as part of the Greek delegation from the United States, and won a bronze medal. Three years later, probably guided by one or another of his stars, he returned to Belgium to participate in another international exhibition in Ghent, brought back a gold medal and met his future wife.

The couple settled down in Ghent, then moved to Brussels where he opened a praline shop on the *rue Marché aux Grains*. Starting in 1935, Leonidas was helped by his nephew, Basile, who quickly succeeded him. He originated the *Leonidas* boutiques as we know them today : small, bright, and with a counter opening out onto the street. This manner of presenting the pralines was, from the beginning, an undeniable advantage since passers-by immediately smelled the aromas from the workshop. And although today the pralines are made in a factory in Anderlecht, much more impersonal, the presentation counters of the shops still give those strolling by a reason to take delight.

At the opening of the XXIst century, *Leonidas* is present from Bolivia to Singapore, and from Oostende to Bastogne.

Just between us...

Some inventions are sometimes the product of unusual or difficult situations. It was thus for the *Leonidas* boutiques. The store on the Boulevard Anspach, rented by Basile Kestekidis, didn't have a door. This arrangement, at the very least bizarre, meant the renter had to enter the premises through the window and use the external window ledge as a sales counter...

A closer look at...

...the *Pearls*. Like those made by oysters, Leonidas' pearls are white (Rum, Champagne, Pistachio, Coconut) or black (Cocoa,

European Pastry Cup 2000

Fine Orange, Amaretto, Whisky).

MARCOLINI (Pierre)

Rue du Bassin Collecteur, 4
1130 Brussels
Tel. 02 216 82 15
Fax 02 216 97 68
Year founded: 1994
Export : confidential
Distribution : 4 stores in Belgium, 1 in Antwerp and since November 2000 1 in Paris

The Selection

As for pralines, *Marcolini* offers more than 70 types, among which we discover some unusual flavours : cinnamon, Earl Grey tea, jasmine, violet, thyme and orange or even ginger.
But the shop's savoir-faire doesn't stop there : four types of *truffés*, *mendiants*, *caraques*, fruit and almond pastes, magnificent cakes and frozen side dishes are also part of the daily selection at Marcolini.

History
Pierre Marcolini is not, strictly speaking, a chocolate maker and it is a little difficult to justify his presence in this guide. But, what do you want, each of us has his little imperfections, and ours in this specific case is to champion the cause, come hell or high water, of *Marcolini*. Because, our man is not, in the final analysis a chocolate artisan ! He's more a true artist, who has earned a seat at the table of the greatest creators in the country, whether they be from culinary, textile or painting circles. Besides, if there was a competition among all the designers in Belgium, he could easily finish among the top in the " All Categories " category.
And those sad spirits can dry their tears ! Be assured, Mesdames and Messieurs, that the author has not been " bought " and hasn't even received one extra penny from his editors to write such commendations. To convince the most sceptical, all it takes is a trip to one of the Master's exhibition galleries (the list is found in the ad hoc chapter...).

European Cup and *Champion of the World*

But *Marcolini* didn't wait for the creation of such an improbable prize to begin gathering the laurels of a glory he well merited. Judge for yourself ! After a " scholarly " stint with some of the greatest (courses at *CERIA* then at the *Infobo* in Uccle, stages at Mahieu, Wittamer and Fauchon...), he gained the prize for the *Best Young Pastry Chef in Belgium* in 1984. A series of other distinctions followed, among which we single out a 1st prize at the *European National Cake Competition*, a Gold Medal at the *National and International Mandarin Napoleon Competition* in 1990 and a Gold Medal at the *Prosper Montagné Competition* in 1991 (best pastry maker in Belgium). He concluded, provisionally, his string of successes with the title of...*World Pastry Champion* at Lyon in 1995 before grabbing, in March 2000 at Rome, the *European Pastry Cup*.
Given these multiple distinctions, it is no wonder that Marcolini is constantly searching for raw ingredients of the finest quality. He defines himself in these terms : " *Arbiter of*

a permanent combat between the ideal and the possible, which tends to tilt the balance towards a perfection that is always just a little too far away for his pleasure. " Along the same idea, Pierre Marcolini thinks that the coating chocolate (*chocolat de couverture)* is the essential point to master in order to obtain a quality product, which means he will always search for a coating chocolate (*chocolat de couverture)* that is, as much as is possible, in harmony with the filling or other aromatic component of his chocolates. Finally, know that he uses up to three different types of cocoa beans to compose what we can definitely call his masterpieces.

A very eclectic artist

The *Marcolini* team, lead by Pierre, his wife Nico and forty others, recently moved to a superb location of 1500m², in Haren, in the area of Bruxelles-Capitale.

There is more than one arrow in Pierre Marcolini's quiver. He also excels in the different related fields of pastry, confectionary, chocolate and ice. In this last category, he is particularly fond of ice sculpture, a practice that is, to say the least, exacting, and he creates the most incredible personalized works. And to return to chocolate, know also that among the most prestigious clients of *Marcolini*, we find Fortis, Peugeot (for the launch of the gleaming 607) and...Delvaux who each commissioned a chocolate in their likeness.

As for Nico, she is, it seems, the "all category" champion of personalised gifts, with a scrupulous eye toward the freshness of the products and she brings particular attention to the presentation. We repeat, these people are artists...

Just between us...

If ever, in the bottom of an old box, you find one or another old *chocolatière* (the utensil, not the wife of a chocolate maker ! *author's note...*) or some old chocolate moulds that you no longer use, send them along to Nico Marcolini. She will certainly be pleased to welcome these fine objects into her personal collection.

MEURISSE

Brusselsesteenweg, 450
1500 Halle
Tel. 02 362 31 11
Fax 02 362 38 40
Year founded: 1845
Distribution : large distribution, 15 % of tablet and bar sales in Belgium

The Selection

Though there is nothing to cause a panic in the world of the classic tablet, let's take another look at the flavours of the filled tablets : raspberry, variegated with raisins, pistachio, vanilla, banana, four fruit and orange. In the filled bars category, there is a new arrival to point out : a bar with macaroons, deliciously crisp and not too sugary. Whereas mini-tablets are offered, rather, in the five conventional flavours, the " Zéro " line and an assortment of pre-packaged pralines bring up the rear.

History

The *Meurisse* chocolate makers – the oldest active Belgian chocolate maker – joined the *Jacobs Suchard Côte d'Or* group in 1986. It is today the second national brand in terms of sales, but isn't marketed abroad. Contrary to *Côte d'Or*, *Meurisse* puts much more emphasis on the taste of the filling ingredients than that of the chocolate.

Advertising contributed enormously to the notoriety of the chocolate maker from Antwerp : we regularly see " Mr. Meurisse " in his television appearances. His method has remained the same over the years : he solicits the input of a clientele well established in his cause before he sets out to " make another... ! ".

A closer look at...

...the *Zéro* bars. Nicknamed the " chocolate filled with cool ", eating it gives a sensation of cold in the mouth. This impression is simply the consequence of a particular recipe for the filling.

NEUHAUS

Postweg, 2
1602 Vlezenbeek
Tel. 02 568 22 11
Fax 02 568 22 07
e-mail : info@neuhaus.be
http://www.neuhaus.be
Year founded: 1857
Export : Neuhaus products are available in 65 countries
Distribution : under any " Neuhaus " sign, specialty shops, pastry shops

The Selection

No amateur of chocolate can be ignorant of the vast array of *Neuhaus* pralines ! Classic but rich, they present a large collection of ganaches, *pralinés*, gianduja and crème fraîches. Among the *Manons*, we point out the presence of two rare exemplars in fondant sugar (vanilla and coffee), in keeping with the original idea. Some *truffés* and a collection of " liqueurs " with impressive labels (J&B, Bisquit, Smirnoff, Cointreau,...) round out the assortment of pralines.

Did you know that, on the other hand, *Neuhaus* also offers ten or so different bars as well as the original tablets, among which we find the Bitter Tea, Milk Hazelnut Nougat, Extra Bitter Orange and Extra Bitter 70% ?

History

In 1857, Jean Neuhaus arrived in Brussels from his native Switzerland. He installed himself in the famous *Galerie de la Reine* (Queen's Gallery) and opened a pharmaceutical confectioner's. His specialities were sweets against coughing, bars of liquorice to appease gastrointestinal problems and even some bitter chocolate tablets. But these were more at home on the " medicine " shelf than with the confections.

The son, Frédéric, when he took over the reins of the store, capitalised on his studies as a master confectioner to progressively replace the medicinal specialties of his father with bonbons of caramel, fruit pastes and other chocolates with vanilla. Business picked up then considerably. At his death in 1912, Jean Neuhaus, grandson of the founder, took over an expanding enterprise.

The beginnings of the praline

The latest Neuhaus was about to revolutionize, maybe even without knowing it, the little world of chocolate making by creating a new treat of filled chocolate that he would name *praline*. This specialty set itself completely apart from the French confection with the same name, invented by the chef of the Duke of Plessis-Praslin. A little while later, the wife of Jean Neuhaus invented the famous *ballotin* box that allows the pralines to be stacked without crushing one another. Having no male descendents, Jean and Louise Neuhaus passed the torch in 1923 to their son-in-law Adelson de Gavre. He was, along with his son, the creator of many pralines. Most of them still exist today, like the *Caprices* and the *Tentations* which, along with a few others, are still made by hand.

The business stayed in the family until 1978, the year when Claude and Jean-Jacques Poncelet took control. They undertook to develop the recognition of *Neuhaus* on the international market over 9 years and re-sold the business in 1987 to the *Tienen Refinery*, the largest Belgian sugar manufacturer. Today, *Neuhaus-Mondose* is integrated in the group *Artal*, to which also belongs the Frenchman *Jeff de Bruges*. But, the purists can put their mind at ease, there is absolutely no question, in Vlezenbeek, of changing habits or jeopardizing the reputation built up by the chocolate maker.

Just between us...

Suzanne Neuhaus, daughter of Jean and Louise and wife of Adelson de Gavre was a famous singer at the no less prestigious *Théâtre Royal de la Monnaie* in Brussels. When she abandoned her public singing she naturally devoted herself to the chocolate maker, to which she was a fundamental support. She was also at the heart of the " Colis de l'amitié "(Care Packages) of chocolate that were sent to expatriated Belgian families in the colonies of central Africa.

A closer look at...

...the " Royales ". Was it the presence of the original store in the "Queen's Gallery" that led *Neuhaus* to offer a series of pralines with the names of several of our kings and queens ? Maybe, but without being able to verify that, we can still state that five contemporary members of the royal family have loaned their name to these chocolate specialties. The *Baudouin* is a " crème fraîche " with butter and vanilla, while the *Fabiola* adds a dark ganache. *Albert* is a *praliné* of toasted hazelnuts dressed in dark chocolate while *Paola* is a body of milk chocolate wrapped around a similar filling to the preceding. Finally, *Astrid* is a gianduja trimmed with butter and candy sugar. And, guess what! Since January 2000, *Philippe et Mathilde* have made their triumphant entry into the *Neuhaus* boutiques under the form of an iron box. It contains photos and pictures from their wedding and, above all, an assortment of 400g (14 oz) of delicious pralines. We understand much easier after all this that *Neuhaus* recently became *Purveyor to the Royal Court*...a truly deserved distinction.

...the *Snobinettes*. No, you are not mistaken, this really does refer to a line of pralines with the *Neuhaus* stamp, and not to some of their more pretentious clients! The *Snobinettes* are four in number (Cappuccino, Irish Coffee, Hazelnut and Champagne). They are small shells of dark chocolate, laced and filled. As for their pretentiousness, it is limited to the fact that we can't help but devour them with our eyes.

Chocolate workshop, middle of the 20th century.

Chocolate everyday

The target products

Though hard chocolate (bars, tablets, pralines,...) is the most demanded and consumed form of chocolate in terms of production, we can't forget the other ways in which chocolate enters our homes. Chocolate is truly an everyday foodstuff, around throughout the day for kids as well as adults, and in a variety of different forms. Curiously, considered by purists as a lesser form, these categories of chocolate products make up at least 50% of the national consumption in many countries. As an example, the very serious Belgian Office of Foreign Commerce (*OBCE*) offers some enlightening figures : 20 kg of chocolate per year per person, if you count all the forms of foodstuffs in which one finds cocoa. The makers have understood this for a long time, publicity campaigns helping along the way.

Cocoa powder

Cocoa liquor is subjected to great pressure (+/- 500 bars) and heated (+/- 100°C). At this time, the cocoa butter is released, and a *tourteau* or cake is formed of the remainder. This very hard puck, about 45 cm in diameter and 5 cm in thickness is almost completely depleted of its fats (between 10 and 20%). It will serve as the basis for the production of cocoa powder. Chocolate makers then have recourse to a process called *alkalisation* or *solubilisation* in which they normally use calcium carbonate as well as soy lecithin. This chemical treatment consists of modifying the pH of the cocoa in order to make it soluble and mellows the flavour.

The last step is called *blutage*. During this stage, the cocoa cake is crushed, pulverized and transformed into a fine powder. In this arena, Belgium distinguishes itself by grinding the cocoa down to 18 microns (sometimes even 12) while Great Britain stops at 24 microns. Take note that the tongue and the palate cannot perceive particles unless smaller than 40 microns. When it contains less than 20% fats, we call it *cocoa maigre* (thin or light cocoa).

We can differentiate among three categories :

pure cocoa, is simply the result of the operations described above and contains no other ingredient. Added to water or milk, it is above all used as a beverage by adults and also serves as the base for various chocolate preparations. It must contain at least 20% fats.

chocolate powder or *sweetened cocoa*, must include a minimum of 32% pure cocoa and only sugar as an additive. Drunk in hot or cold milk, it is principally a treat for the young, especially at breakfast.

chocolate preparations' cocoa content falls below 32% and they often contain other ingredients like cereals, malt, flours, powdered milk, etc. They are also found on the breakfast table where they provide the necessary energy for the day. The "star " is of course *Nesquik*, which has been the best selling soluble "cocoa" in the world for the past thirty years. In Belgium and in France, it represents about 50% of the market sector. As for others, we also place in this category *Poulain Grand Arôme*, *Ovomaltine* and *Banania*. This chocolaty banana powder, today losing some of its steam, was the first of all the modern cocoa powders. Launched in 1914 with much publicity, it has often been imitated, but never equalled.

Cocoa powder also serves as a base for ready-made milk preparations that we find in supermarkets and cafes. This category seems to be contracting when compared to the others.

The « candy-bars »

It is, simply, one of the shining categories of the chocolate world, if you just look at the revenues that it generates. In Belgium alone, we count 24.000 tonnes consumed annually. Like cocoa, this type of chocolate delicacy comes from across the Atlantic, to be more precise, from the United States, which remains among the principle producers. On the European level, Switzerland probably finishes first in this category, with the varieties from *Milka* and *Nestlé*. As for traditional chocolate makers, they have also filled out their "collections" and offer several types of chocolate (dark, milk, white,...) while the fillings have multiplied, no longer limited to the traditional *hazelnut* or *praliné*.

The principle brands, in no particular order, are named *Milky-Way*, *Mars*, *Twix*, *Kit-Kat*, *Lion*, *Snickers* and *Bounty*. They are the object of a veritable media battle and thanks to the "young and dynamic" image they promote, they are associated with every event of any size in the world.

Energy to spare...

« Candy-bars » all contain ingredients not found in the traditional bars. Most often found are things like caramel, puffed rice, biscuit, peanuts, coconut and nougat. The part that is strictly chocolate is generally small, and isn't more than one among many ingredients of the confection. And so, it is toward these makers that the detractors of the new European directive cast their gaze, making their case understood that these powerful multinationals now have the green light to again reduce their production costs with the law on their side.

The principle competition for these "unusual" products is found on both the side of the traditional filled bar makers and the side of other treats without cocoa, but with the same energetic image (for example, *Granny* or *Balisto*).

Classified in a related category, confections such as *Smarties*, *M&M's*, *Rolo* or *Chokotoff* also are benefiting from a never before seen level of popularity, principally among young consumers.

Chocolate desserts

To list here every ready-made dessert that contains chocolate would be impossible. The shelves of the super- and hyper-markets overflow with this type of good. As a reminder, we had to site the ubiquitous creams and chocolate mousses that continue to please children and grown-ups.

In the last few years certain other targeted products have appeared in individual portions in the refrigerated cases of larger stores. We point out *Delhaize Le Lion* who offers, under their own label, *tiramisu*, *profiteroles* and other chocolate delicacies.

The bread spreads

An indispensable element of breakfast for most families, this represents about 0,6% of the average monthly budget for Belgian households, who are the largest European consumers. Here, the situation is relatively simple because the market is largely dominated by *Nutella*, the hazelnut spread from the Italian group *Ferrero*. Other brands exist, but they only scrounge the crumbs, something which says nothing about their quality. It rather seems that *Nutella*, with the help of intensive publicity, has become the bread spread that "children recommend to their parents".

But although *Nutella* sticks by its mix of milk and hazelnuts that made its success, the competition hasn't been asleep. Just as an example, *Milky-Way* offers a spread combining white and milk chocolate, while *Kwatta* markets a *Double Milk* as well as a delicious dark chocolate named simply *Pure*.

We would also point out that numerous small artisans exist who market "*de luxe*" bread spreads agreeably packaged, with incomparable flavours, and whose prices range more in the "gift" category. In this niche we suggest (why not) *Charlemagne* from Belgium and *Beussent* from France. On the other hand, this « choco » spread that is eaten daily is probably the most economical way to enjoy chocolate...and to introduce it to children.

Special occasions

The simple fact of pronouncing the word « chocolate » inescapably evokes exotic thoughts full of images of sun and pleasure. Rapidly, we also think of the special occasions with which it is associated. Because choco-

late, and by extension cocoa, is one of the rare alimentary products in regular consumption that provokes as much desire as it does pleasure. Of course, other products evoke special occasions, but there are very few regular consumers of oysters, champagne, *foie-gras* or caviar. This is one of the paradoxes of chocolate : it is eaten and offered all year long, but remains quasi indispensable at celebrations as well.

There are two principle periods associated with it : Easter and Christmas. Belgian children wouldn't forget to add *Saint-Nicolas* and lovers would hold it against us if we forgot Saint Valentine's day.

And since the twelfth month of the year is certainly the one when we make and eat the most chocolate in many countries, some chocolate makers have profited from this by specialising in this niche (and capitalizing on Sant's advertising). We note as examples *Italo-Suisse* in Belgium and the fabulous *Fleuriste du Chocolat* in France.

Saint Nicolas and Santa Claus

The month of December is of course a very festive period. From the beginning of the month, patronal festivals signal it, and it runs for several animated weeks...full of good chocolaty moments !

The earliest beneficiaries are certainly the Belgian children. The 6th of December, Saint-Nicolas (never call him *Santa Claus*, he can't stand it...) accompanied by his donkey, comes to every house in the night to distribute toys and goodies. Among these, pieces and figurines of moulded chocolate certainly rank number one. To such a point in fact, that it is easy to imagine the increase in production required to cover this generous distribution. Don't they say, in some regions, when the sky reddens the evenings before the big night that Saint-Nicolas must surely be *cooking his chocolates* ?

A worldwide phenomenon

Less than three weeks later, another character enters the scene. The debonair Santa Claus, accompanied by his yoke of reindeer and his sleigh, comes and leaves presents and sweets at the foot of the pine tree that bears his name. And, maybe because he is braver (or better advertised) than his Belgian colleague, his territory is considerably larger.

Many children around the world wait for the 25th of December with a certain impatience and the jovial bearded one, dressed all in red, is also represented in multiple chocolate forms.

But, if Christmas is a time reserved for children, the "grown-ups" enjoy it just as much. In fact, 93% of the French consider it traditional to eat chocolate during the occasion, while 66% find it unavoidable during the same period.

And while the Europeans have developed the habit of savouring a traditional chocolate Yule log dessert during Christmas, the Mexicans have for themselves, at Christmas Eve supper, a stuffed turkey (a species that is definitely at risk during this period...) coated with chocolate...

Easter

Of all the occasions during which we eat chocolate, Easter is probably the most open to the talents of the chocolate makers. In fact, there appear at this time a good number of montages, often well executed, that incorporate bunnies and chicks.

We find these animals, accompanied by chickens, lambs and fish in the form of moulded elements. This tradition dates back to the XIXth century (1830) and is possible thanks to the evolution of the technique.

But what would Easter be without its little eggs ? Filled or not, they please children and those who remain like children. Because everyone knows that the eggs that we find Easter morning in the garden are delivered each year from Rome by the bells returning from their pilgrimage to the holy city. Whether of industrial or artisan quality, they are, over a period of days, separated brutally and finally from their aluminium wrapping to come to an end in the gourmand's mouth. A kind of mini-*bouchée*, their fillings have probably been more original in recent years (orange, puffed rice, biscuit,...) and are becoming more and more like little pralines.

Are they going to ring the bells ?

To close this chapter, we are allowing ourselves to point out two fairly sombre points.
The first concerns, once again, the infamous vegetable fats. Mass production, required by the intensive distribution of these bells, definitely tempts the manufacturers to start down that path, if they haven't already done so.
The second deals with distribution. We know for certain that during this period, the bells have such a considerable amount of work to do that they couldn't possibly – even though they would like to – supply all of their vendors on the Easter weekend. But is this sufficient reason to start cramming the shelves in the supermarkets beginning in February ? It seems, anyway, that the question runs the risk of finding its answer in legislation...

Christmas atmosphere.

Chocolate in cuisine

The "grand classics"

Once we look into the question, we see immediately that chocolate is a quasi-inescapable element of desserts and sweet side dishes. Preparations containing chocolate always get more votes, and are always greeted with a smile by your guests. Does maybe the delicate scent of chocolate bring old memories of childhood back to the surface ... ?

Alexandra Cocktail

To make this traditional cocktail, mix in a shaker with ice *1/3 crème fraîche fleurette, 1/3 crème de cocoa and 1/3 cognac* (or alternatively gin). Shake vigorously and serve over cracked ice.

Chocolate mousse

Serves 4 :
3 eggs, 200g dark chocolate, 30g butter, 125g confectioner's sugar,

1 pinch of salt.
Break the chocolate into pieces, put it into a bowl with a tablespoon of water and melt in a bain-marie. Add the butter and stir to get a smooth mixture.
In a terrine, beat the egg yolks and sugar together until they become light in colour. Next add the melted chocolate and mix again, finally incorporate the egg

Chocolate mousse: how delightful!

whites after they have been beaten until stiff, along with a pinch of salt.
With a wooden spatula, lift the mixture from the bottom to obtain a consistent mixture without breaking the egg whites.
Dispense into individual serving dishes and refrigerate for a minimum of three hours.
A widely used recipe, inspired by the book "Cuisine pour toute l'année - M. Maine"

Chocolate "Biscuit"

Serves 6 :
200g sugar, 6 eggs + 2 whites, 25g flour, 25g starch, 25g cocoa.
Preheat the oven to 180°C (thermostat 6) and during this time, butter a cake mould.
Mix the eggs and whites with the sugar. Warm it for 1 minute in a bain-marie, then beat with an electric mixer until a homogenous mixture is attained.
Sift together the cocoa, starch and flour. Add it to the other ingredients.
Pour into the mould and bake for 25 minutes. Un-mould the cake while still warm.

Chocolate cake

For an 8 inch diameter cake :

6 eggs, 250g sugar, 250g cooking chocolate (fondant), 100g powdered almonds, 250g butter, 3 tablespoons starch, 2 packets of vanilla sugar, 1/2 teaspoon yeast, 125g eating chocolate, 100g caster sugar

Beat the egg yolks with the sugar until they lighten in colour and form ribbons. In a casserole, break up the 250g of chocolate and add 2 tablespoons of water. Place the casserole in a bain-marie, hot but not boiling.

Next, add the sifted almond powder, yeast, starch and finally the vanilla sugar. Incorporate the 200g of softened, but not melted, butter, 3 egg whites beaten until stiff and a pinch of salt.

Work the mixture by delicately lifting so as not to break the egg whites. Pour into a mould that has been greased and sprinkled with the caster sugar. Fill to a level leaving around 1 cm at the top and place in an oven that has preheated for about 20 minutes (thermostat 6-7). Bake for 25 to 30 minutes.

Take the cake out and let it cool slightly before un-moulding. Let it cool completely on a metal rack.

For the icing, use the eating chocolate, melted in the bain-marie. Turn it in a casserole just until it forms an appropriate consistency. Finish by coating the cake with the help of a spatula.

Hint : the quicker the cake cooks, the more its centre will retain a creamy and smooth texture.

Coffee-Chocolate Charlotte

Serves 6 :

36 "Cuiller" biscuits, 300g "Dessert" chocolate, 8 eggs, 45cl very strong coffee, 75g caster sugar, 1 pinch of salt

Break the chocolate into pieces and let it melt in a bain-marie. Away from the heat source, add the strong coffee while stirring.

Separate the whites from the yolks of the eggs and incorporate the yolks one at a time. Next, add the caster sugar and whites that have been beaten until stiff with the salt.

In a Charlotte mould, cover the sides and bottom with the "Cuiller" biscuits. Delicately pour the mixture over the biscuits and cover (with a plate).

Place in the refrigerator for approximately 12 hours, then un-mould the Charlotte onto a plate.

Filled Easter eggs

Fills 6 eggs :

6 empty eggs, 6 egg yolks, 200g dark baker's chocolate, 200g butter, 25 cl crème fraîche, 100g sugar, orange (or vanilla) extract.

Make a small hole in the ends of each of the six eggs (raw and fresh, of course). Delicately enlarge the hole on the pointy end and blow to remove the contents.

Melt the chocolate broken into pieces with a tablespoon of milk over a very low flame. Stir constantly. Add the melted butter, the cream, sugar and flavouring orange (or vanilla) extract.

Stir continuously until very smooth.

Belgian stamps 1999

Fill each hollowed eggshell with the help of piping nozzle and cover the holes with small pieces of shell. Let harden in the refrigerator for 24 hours.
Adaptation of a classic Easter Sunday recipe.

Chocolate soufflé

Serves 4 :
90g chocolate, 2 egg yolks and 5 whites, 80g sugar plus 2 tablespoons, 4 tablespoons milk, 20g butter, icing sugar
Butter small individual moulds (ramekins) and sprinkle with two tablespoons of sugar. Place them in the refrigerator.
Preheat the oven during the rest of the preparation (thermostat 8).
Break the chocolate into pieces and let it melt in a bain-marie. Next, add to it 60g sugar and 4 tablespoons milk. Mix together just until you get a homogenous mixture. Let this cool slightly.
Separate the whites from the egg yolks, then incorporate the yolks with the mixture while constantly whisking. Beat the 5 egg whites until stiff and then add the remaining 20g of sugar. Little by little, delicately incorporate the eggs into the cooled chocolate cream. Divide the mixture among the ramekins, sprinkle with icing sugar and bake for approximately 15 minutes. Serve hot from the oven.

Chocolate truffles

385 grams of UHT cream, 465 grams bitter chocolate 70%, 75 grams butter, cocoa powder.
Boil the cream and pour it over the grated bitter chocolate. Add the butter after being whipped. Let the mixture stiffen in the refrigerator until it has the appropriate consistency.
Next, form small truffles with the help of a ladle. Finally, roll the truffles in the cocoa powder. As a variation, you may mix confectioner's sugar with ground coffee and use it as a coating. Keep these in a cold and dry environment.
"Palet d'Or" truffle recipe from Pierre Marcolini

Original recipes, or recipes from elsewhere

Though the first words that come automatically to mind are "dessert" and "sugar" when one thinks of cooking with chocolate, it (or more often cocoa used without the addition of sugar) offers many other applications, frequently practised in other latitudes.

The Mexicans, the "inventors" of cocoa, have regaled for generations with the famous "*Poblano Mole*". It uses a sauce that mixes chocolate infused with cinnamon and various peppers. Usually served on turkey or chicken, this accompaniment is a deep brown colour and, it seems, makes the locals salivate with just the mention of its name.

For some time, a few of our great Western chefs have recently taken up the game and have since created numerous original recipes using cocoa. This has led to a point where we can easily conceive a meal entirely composed of dishes that incorporate cocoa, from the aperitif right through to the after dinner coffee. Are you a little queasy at the prospect ? Well don't be. In fact, at the risk of being repetitious, its not a questions of over sugared dishes, but rather cocoa used as a spice in an overall dish, along the lines of say, cinnamon or vanilla.

Cocoa bubble

8 measure white *crème de cacao*, 2 measures pear *eau de vie*, finished with Perrier

Created at the "Le Forum" bar — 4, boulevard Malesherbes 75008 Paris

Cocoa soup

Serves 4 to 6 :

1 large white of leek, 1/2 courgette, 100 to 150g celeriac, 1 medium onion, extra virgin olive oil, chicken stock, 50g peanuts (roasted and salted), 2 squares extremely dark chocolate, 2 to 3 dl crème fraîche, fresh ground black pepper, fleur de se (salt)l.

Wash and trim the vegetables, chop to a small dice. Place them all into a pot and sweat them in a little oil.

When the vegetables are tender and sweated, add enough chicken stock just to cover them. Next, add the peanuts and let this cook for 20 minutes.

Add the two squares of chocolate, let them melt and stir them in. Taste the soup and add salt if necessary for seasoning. Finally, pass the soup through a *chinoise* and re-heat.

Beat the crème fraîche with salt and pepper for seasoning and place a dollop in the centre of the dish filled with soup.

Recipe from the Chocolaterie Galler

Carbonades My Way

Serves 6 :

1kg beef shoulder, 1 litre gueuze (Belgian beer), 2 slices ginger bread, 6 large onions, 2 tablespoons flour, thyme, bay laurel, 50g butter, 1 tablespoon Dijon mustard, salt, pepper, 2 squares chocolate

Cut the meat into large cubes and brown in a stew pot. Add the thyme, bay laurel and minced onions. Salt, pepper and flour.

In a saucepan, let the chocolate melt in a little of the gueuze. Dilute the mustard with a little of the gueuze. Crumble the gingerbread very finely.

When the meat and onions are well browned, deglaze the pan with the remaining gueuze. Let this reduce. Then add the mustard, chocolate and gingerbread.

Stir occasionally with a wooden spoon. Let cook covered, over a low heat for 80 minutes. Serve in the cooking vessel, accompanied by a Saint-Estèphe *Château Montrose*, by a *Moulin à Vent Domaine de la Tour du Bief* or…a gueuze.

Recipe from Michel David - "La Béguine des Béguines" Restaurant in Bruxelles

Chocolate Pumpkin Cake

Serves 4 to 6 :

450 g pumpkin, 150g dark chocolate, 120g "Carnation" unsweetened concentrated milk, 3 eggs, 75g powdered sugar, 2 tablespoons flour, 25g butter.

Gently melt the chocolate in a bain-marie. During this time, preheat the oven (thermostat 6-7).

Mix the sugar, flour and eggs, gently add the milk. Next, add the melted dark chocolate and vigorously beat into a batter.

Prepare a slice of the pumpkin by peeling and grating it into fine strings (as for a carrot salad). Add 3/4 of the pumpkin to the preparation.

In a buttered square dish, place the mixture and cover it with the grated pumpkin. Place the dish in the oven and let bake for 30 minutes.

Turn out the cake only after it has completely cooled.

This cake is particularly enjoyed by children around Halloween.

Chocolate Fondue

Chocolate fondue, like its cheesy cousin, doesn't come from Switzerland. It is not yet a culinary classic, but no doubt its popularity will grow in the coming years. As proof, the growing number of "fondue" restaurants or traditional restaurants that offer it on their menus, and the ready made preparations available at the supermarkets. Easy to make yourself, and as convivial as its older relative, it will probably be a must-have in the XXIst century to come.

It has the advantage of being agreeable in all seasons and goes very well with all kinds of fruit. It is best to avoid certain fruits with pips and to peel others, like citrus fruits. The smallest can be served whole and others cut into cubes, sticks or quartered, in rounds or shaved, according to their texture and size.

Serves 4 to 6 :

500g dark chocolate, 125g crème fraîche, 500 ml milk.

Gently melt the chocolate in the mixture of milk and cream. As for the classic fondue, place this on the table over a heat source (for example in a fondue pot) and accompany with fondue forks.

Serve with chopped fresh fruit and little morsels of cake (Savoie, Génoise,…) lightly dried, or brioche bread.

You can adjust the preparation by adding to the mixture 1 or 2

tablespoons of sugar (or butter) to sweeten, a few tablespoons of very strong coffee to give body and even infuse it with a vanilla bean broken in two.

Matching chocolate to a beverage

Ever since chocolate came in through the front door of the culinary world, no rule aimed at definitively fixing an appropriate beverage, whatever that might be, has really reached unanimity.

In the "zero risk" category, water is a natural choice. There is no danger of it interacting with the chocolate, whether it is black, milk or white. It has the advantage of erasing the impressions left behind on the palate, and its thirst quenching properties need no explanation. It even helps if it is warm, to enhance the delivery of the flavours developed by the chocolate. But what gourmet, no matter how much of a purist, is passionate about mineral water... ?

Coffee and tea, whichever you are fond of, seem to create a sort of osmosis with chocolate. The drink, boiling hot and taken in small consecutive sips, multiplies the aroma and flavour of the chocolate, while the chocolate, if we dare to dip it for an instant into the cup, better exhales its olfactory and gustative properties. One should tend toward dark chocolate with an *arabica* or a *robusta*, coffees with a pronounced bitterness, while those who prefer tea should choose an *Earl Grey* or a *Darjeeling*, very tannic. Milk chocolate goes better with a dessert coffee or a fruity or floral infusion. But, coffee and tea are still considered lesser beverages in the gastronomic world, and goes better as the close to an excellent family meal than to interfere among the service at a high class meal.

In the realm of the sommelier, the divergence of attitudes are much clearer and even seem to divide the specialists.

Champagne, the wine of kings and king of wines for many amateurs, seems to get along fairly poorly with chocolate. Only Robert Linxe recommends it, to accompany certain chocolate desserts like ice creams and sorbets. He prefers, like most of his colleagues, to associate sweet wines like *Muscat de Rivesaltes* or the *Banyuls* with his cakes filled with ganache. These beverages, to which we should add *Maury,* are on the other hand unanimous among the oenophiles.

The association of dark chocolate with "classic" red wines takes on more subjective characteristics. As a general rule, they get along poorly with cocoa...and it is not rare to find the gustative particularities of them neutralising one another rather than enhancing. Only the very tannic *crus* satisfy the taste buds, and in this group the Bordeaux – and in particular Médoc – seems the best suited, as the Belgian chocolate maker Druart likes to point out. We would also add certain wines from the South-West, among which we will place the Cahors at the top of the list. Milk chocolate goes fairly well with Beaujolais, lighter and fresher.

Maury: the region of a great wine

Coffee, Liqueurs and Eaux-de-vie

Otherwise, dry white wines are precluded without hesitation, but a few might recommend testing the harmonies with one or another Alsatian wine (Gewüztraminer or Sylvaner especially) or, a braver step according to us, with the famous yellow wine of Jura.

But the true perfect compliment, which needs no argument, is chocolate and alcohols. Liqueurs and eaux-de-vie are in fact the perfect allies of chocolate, in whatever form, though the odds on favourite is with small squares of very dark chocolate and with dessert. In this camp, the priority goes to Whisky and Cognac while the pear eaux-de-vie (Poire Williams) or the kirsches are equally marvellous. And to support our contention, we point out the numerous cocktails based on cocoa, including the famous *Alexandra* (see above).

Finally, at a time when it is slipping more and more any to the hallowed halls of the culinary art, how could we forget about beer ? Though the marriage of the two might seem a little "arranged", it isn't unconsummated at any rate, always provoking mixed emotions. It would suffice to convince oneself by trying the union of a square of milk chocolate with a nice "Abbaye" brown ale or a "Trappiste " ale or even a stout (Guiness), while the harmony between dark chocolate and the strong blonds called "Triples" provokes extreme sensations. As for desserts, especially those that also contain fresh fruit, matching them with a Gueuze could be the beginning of a long and beautiful romance.

But all this goes back as much to personal tastes as to any pure theory. All amateurs of chocolate have, on one day or another, bitten into a square or taken their dessert while finishing off the last of the wine from the meal. And the truly ideal association must be tailored to each personality, let yourself go and never hesitate to try new experiences...you'll only find yourself more satisfied for it !

Good wine and great chocolate: the perfect harmony

Chocolate
and
health

Since Europe discovered chocolate in the XVIth century, an enormous amount has been written and said on the subject. Held up to public obloquy by its detractors, chocolate sometimes suffered considerations that were crazy to say the least. Put on a pedestal by its adoring fans, it regularly benefits from an unequalled aura for a product of daily consumption.

Beyond the indescribable pleasure of tasting a morsel of chocolate, is it a necessary aliment to a balanced diet, or a sweet like all the others ? We had to wait for the XXth century, and the development of science, in order to have the first elements of our response. Curiously, it is also after the Second World War that chocolate was accused of a series of misdeeds for which it is absolutely not responsible.

At the end of the XIXth century and the beginning of the following, chocolate was regularly used as a pharmaceutical, along with plants and other elements that weren't always really medicinal. Supposed to cure an incredible list of ills, it was above all used to mask the heavy taste of certain other ingredients. On the other hand, since Napoleon the 1st up to the wars waged in the 90's by the American army, chocolate has always been an integral part of the troops' daily rations.

Today, at the beginning of the third millennium, new studies regularly come out to corroborate a fact that is now accepted: chocolate has more qualities than faults.

Truths and tales

Chocolate is a source of energy

TRUE : Dark chocolate is rich in magnesium (112 mg/100g), potassium (365 mg/100g) and phosphorus (173 mg/100g). Milk chocolate adds calcium (200 mg pour 100g). We also find traces of iron, sodium, fluoride and copper. It also contains vitamins (B, B2, PP) and represents a non-negligible part of the daily ration of lipids, glucides, protides, and fibre. To a slightly lesser degree for white chocolate, since it contains no...cocoa. An excellent re-energizer for after intense physical effort because its total caloric value is 500 kcal/100g. Chocolate is as important to intellectual activities of long durations. Better than crib-notes, a chocolate bar with hazelnuts ?

Chocolate contributes to weight gain

TRUE and FALSE : A reasonable consumption of chocolate after a meal (1 or 2 squares) wouldn't lead to any significant weight gain. But, because of its high level of fats and its low aptitude for digestion after a copious meal, it is not suggested to consume it under those conditions when dieting to lose weight. So be forewarned : its

However, chocolate is good for health.
and what's more, it's a powerful aphrodisiac!
Oh yes !?!
ZACK

dangerous to confuse « *Noir de Noir* » and « *Weight Watchers* »...

Chocolate is responsible for crises de foie (liver crises – bilious attack)

FALSE : the term « *crise de foie* » being inappropriate, and existing in no other language than French, we could only accuse chocolate of causing digestive problems when consumed in too great a quantity. Nevertheless, no scientific study has ever been completed on the liver function of subjects who abuse pralines filled with whisky on a daily basis...

Chocolate causes cavities

FALSE : no real risk has ever been proven as long as a good dental hygiene regimen is followed. In addition, chocolate contains substances that fight cavities, like fluoride, tannins and phosphates. So now we can tell you that you needn't always associate drilling with chocolate...

Chocolate is responsible for skin allergies

TRUE and FALSE : We can't say it enough, cocoa can not be held responsible for attacks of acne, nor for other allergic reactions. A study of 383 people susceptible to food allergies showed that chocolate was implicated in only 0,8% of the cases. We fear that it is the elements contained in the chocolate (soy, milk proteins,...) rather than the cocoa itself that are at the root of the allergic reactions. Further to this point, the addition of other vegetable fats in chocolate could have unforeseen consequences. In effect, in the absence of correct labelling concerning the exact nature of the vegetable fats, we cannot exclude the appearance of skin problems in some consumers whose digestive systems would not assimilate one or another of the oils consumed along with the *new* chocolate.

Chocolate protects the cardiovascular system

TRUE : a recent study (July 2000) published by an American university tends to show that a moderate and regular consumption of chocolate could have beneficial effects on long term health, the same as green tea or wine. Other analysis has

Extract of the children's paper "Tintin", 1950
(the elephant Mr. Cotdor symbolises the "Côte d'Or" chocolate factory)

shown that 40g of dark chocolate deliver the same beneficial effects as a glass of red wine. It's diverse elements protect the heart from blood clots, inhibit plaque formation and reduce the risk of coronary thrombosis in subjects that do not smoke and are in good health. In addition, chocolate contains flavanoids, substances with antioxidant properties also found in aspirin, as well as traces of sterotonin, which controls the regulation of arterial hypertension. So, which is better : a nice daily glass of wine and a chocolate bar starting in youth, or the infamous regulatory medicines and a triple bypass surgery at fifty ?

Chocolate is prohibited for diabetics

FALSE : sugar (sucrose) added to cocoa in the making of chocolate is sometimes replaced by fructose or by maltose (sugar contained in germinated barley) which can be assimilated by diabetics. The change in flavour can hardly be discerned. Some praline makers have even followed the path of the chocolate makers and produce pralines that contain no sucrose. Note however that this chocolate is not less caloric than the one manufactured in the traditional manner : fats are often added to facilitate the fabrication.

Extract of the children's paper "Tintin", 1950

Chocolate is a drug

FALSE : consumption of chocolate doesn't provoke any of the symptoms that drug taking does : withdrawals or increased cravings and consumption. And though it is true that cocoa contains substances (anandamides) that are contained in cannabis, a man of 60 kg (130 lbs) would have to consume 11 kg (24.25 lbs) per day to get the same effects. Given the weight gain that this would cause, one would imagine it easier to make a weekly round trip to Amsterdam …

Chocolate increases "cholesterol"

TRUE and FALSE : dark chocolate has an insignificant amount of cholesterol, on the order of 1,3mg/100g. On the other hand, the fatty acids present in cocoa butter have the ability to lower the LDL cholesterol level (the one that is bad for our body) without diminishing the level of HDL cholesterol, which has a beneficial effect. As for milk chocolate and pralines, the milk or cream that they contain can lead to a rise in bad cholesterol.

Chocolate causes constipation

FALSE : 100g of cocoa contains as much fibre as 100g of whole grain bread, that is, 9 grams. Consumption of chocolate then contributes to the good working of the intestinal track. In addition, the more cocoa chocolate contains, the less sugar, an element that interrupts intestinal functions. A tip : *Danone* should come up with a chocolate version of *Actimel*...

Chocolate causes euphoria

TRUE : Besides its other substances, cocoa contains theobromine (an alkaloid stimulant) and caffeine. Cocoa then has a tonic effect on the central nervous system and we can confirm that it improves those functions. Moreover, cocoa also reduces stress or anxiety and is also a notable antidepressant,

thanks to the phenylethylamine that it contains. And for premenstrual women, there is sugar to replenish her deficiency. This is no doubt why we dive again and again into chocolate : it has substances that are necessary for good balance in our bodies. From a strictly energy point of view, we also note that chocolate is rich is sugars that assimilate easily into the body, something that allows us to easily get over those little pangs of hunger.

Chocolate is an aphrodisiac

TRUE and FALSE : no serious study has ever demonstrated that chocolate might have any aphrodisiac qualities. But, popular rumour says otherwise since the beginning of time, so to be sure, we should (re)test this idea!!

Amusing properties attributed to chocolate over the centuries

Different regions of the world, and different ages, have attributed an impressive series of properties to chocolate, they are sometimes amusing and sometimes effective.

In the age of the Mayas, cocoa butter was, among other things, employed as a preventative against snakebites, or to heal the liver and lungs. The "Indians" also imagined that they would encounter fewer dangers if they had drunk a cup in the morning.

Having arrived in Europe, it was quickly made the object of a medical treatise that is original, to say the least. Augustin Farfan, doctor to Philippe II of Spain, published in 1579 that « *two cocoas roasted and ground fine can be used to heal chapping on the tips of the breasts* ». In this same work, one can read that « *chocolate taken very hot in the morning is a good purgative for those who suffer from a constriction of the abdomen* ».

In the XVIIIth century, Spanish women thought that chocolate caused weight loss. For this reason, they had it served in impressive quantities : the heaviness of stomach that it caused effectively made them lose their appetite. Those who breakfast on " non-fat cottage cheese – toast – non-fat margarine " should maybe think about it...

As for the celebrated gastronome Brillat-Savarin, wasn't it he who said «...*all men of spirit who feel they have become temporarily sluggish ... that all men who think the air heavy, the time passing slow and the atmosphere difficult to abide... that all these should administer to themselves a good half-litre of warm chocolate and all will seem marvellous.* » ?

Accursed Aphrodite...

We have also seen above that chocolate was available in the pharmacies of the XIXth century. We would notably point out chocolate with ground acorn to combat the lack of *vitality*, a chocolate purgative and another supposed to battle...venereal diseases. Note an amusing detail in this : the cocoa that was lauded at this time as a sexual stimulant was also supposed to assuage the health problems due to abuses in that realm. A most original method to fight fire with fire...

As a conclusion, let us return for an instant to these pretended aphrodisiac virtues. Whatever the scientific truths are, we can confirm that in centuries past chocolate became one of the key instruments of a certain lewdness. We site most notably the example of Madame du Barry, long-time « favorite » of Louis XV, who made all her lovers drink a large cup of chocolate... We can easily understand then why, in 1624, Franciscus Rauch, theologian, disapproved of the use of chocolate in convents, declaring that it « *heated the spirit and the passions* ».

Index

Bibliography

LINXE R., La Maison du Chocolat, Robert Laffont, 1992.

COADY Ch., Les Meilleurs Chocolats et Chocolatiers, Hermé, 1995.

COLLECTIF, Le Livre du Chocolat, Flammarion, 1995.

MOMMAERTS M., L'Aventure du Chocolat Belge, J.M. Collet, 1997.

MERCIER J., Chocolat Belge, La Renaissance du Livre, 1997.

TEUBNER Ch., Le Chocolat, Nathan, 1997.

Guide des Croqueurs de Chocolat, Stock, 1998.

BOURRE J.M., De l'Epi à la Bière, Flammarion, 2000.

Mes Secrets Chocolat, Editions Soumillion, Bruxelles, 2000.

Personal notes:

Personal notes:

Personal notes:

Personal notes:

Personal notes:

Personal notes: